Sasthak Sabarat

D0094101

EDITED BY
SUSAN REYNOLDS

Sasthak Sabarat
Baathak

MY DAD IS MY HERO

Tributes to the Men Who Gave Us
Life, Love, and Driving Lessons

Adamsmedia

AVON, MASSACHUSETTS

Published by
Adams Media, a division of F+W Media, Inc.
57 Littlefield Street, Avon, MA 02322. U.S.A.
www.adamsmedia.com

ISBN 10: 1-59869-794-3
ISBN 13: 978-1-59869-794-0

Printed in the United States of America.

J I H G F E D C B A

Library of Congress Cataloging-in-Publication Data
is available from the publisher.

This publication is designed to provide accurate and authoritative information
with regard to the subject matter covered. It is sold with the understanding that
the publisher is not engaged in rendering legal, accounting, or other professional advice. If legal advice or other expert assistance is required, the services of
a competent professional person should be sought.

—From a *Declaration of Principles* jointly adopted by a Committee of the
American Bar Association and a Committee of Publishers and Associations

Many of the designations used by manufacturers and sellers to distinguish their
product are claimed as trademarks. Where those designations appear in this
book and Adams Media was aware of a trademark claim, the designations have
been printed with initial capital letters.

This book is available at quantity discounts for bulk purchases.
For information, please call 1-800-289-0963.

I lovingly dedicate this anthology to my brothers,
James Lamar Reynolds and Roy Joseph Reynolds,
who are two of the best fathers I know.

Also to my adopted spiritual father, poet Robert Bly,
from whom I learned to recognize and appreciate
the gifts a father brings.

And to my Uncle John Lyle, the beloved patriarch
of the Reynolds family, and to my son, who I firmly believe will
be an excellent father some day.

Acknowledgments

At Adams Media, I'd like to thank Director of Innovation Paula Munier for her enthusiasm and generosity in helping birth projects; associate editor Brendan O'Neill; editorial assistant Sara Stock; and everyone else involved at Adams. And, of course, I owe a big thank you to the fifty contributors who shared their touching stories for all of us to enjoy! Thank you for honoring the fathers who nurtured and inspired you, and who will now enrich all our lives.

Contents

Introduction

Fathers are mythological and psychological giants within a family, and a nation. A healthy father protects, guides, instructs, nurtures, and adores his children. He would be both wise and affectionate; both spontaneous and dutiful; both gentle and strong. An ideal father would sense what his children needed and then seek a way to provide it—and I don't mean physical needs as much as psychological or ideological or spiritual needs. Unlike mothers, fathers are bonded by affection, more than biology. Fathers welcome children into their world, and later introduce their children to the larger world. A healthy father supports his children in becoming whom they most want to be.

Healthy fathers also model strength, tenacity, determination, industry, generosity, devotion, and even romance. All children need a father, and the lucky ones end up with a father that meets—and often exceeds—their emotional, psychological, intellectual, biological, and spiritual needs. And it's never too late.

Like Priscilla Carr ("More Than Mentors: Providential Dads"; page 223), I, too, found a father substitute in the form of poet Robert Bly.

I first encountered Robert Bly at a small writing conference in Northern California, and then proceeded to attend the same weekend conference three years in a row, mostly to be in his presence, to absorb aspects of his character. Still, I almost keeled over when Bly first spoke directly to me. He had no idea how much his mere presence had proved balm to my father wounds. He was re-fathering our entire nation at the time, offering workshops for men, peaking around the time of his bestselling book, *Iron John*. Bly provided an image that I could sink my teeth into; a vision of a father that both inspired and validated me. And he did it without even knowing much about me, or how deeply his actions and words impacted me. He was simply out in the world being fully himself, fully present, sensitive, kind, generous, strong, poetic, and brilliant. I snapped a photograph of him during one of those conferences, framed it, and kept it on my desk for many years. When anyone asked who he was, I always answered "my spiritual father."

I also had a friend's father step up in a very concrete way ("The Colonel to the Rescue"; page 139), and, again, he had no real idea at the time how much it meant to me, how much his mere presence strengthened me, nor how much his wisdom guided me through some dark and difficult days. But the fathers I admire most are my two brothers, Jim and Roy Reynolds. Despite our mutual lack of effectual fathering, both of my brothers gleefully embraced fatherhood. Oddly enough, both spent several years in the roles of Mr. Mom, and both proved exceptionally nurturing, kind, and devoted. On Father's Day, it's them I think of fondly; the way they love their children has long impressed me.

In the following fifty stories, you will meet many fathers, all of who had a major impact on their children's lives. Some are World War II or Vietnam veterans, though even those soldiers are honored for their gentle spirits; some are farmers or mailmen or laborers or woodworkers or writers; some are football players or sportsmen; and some are a stepdad or grandfather who stepped up to father. All impressed their children with their integrity, their humor, their charm, their loyalty, their imagination, their fortitude, and their dreams, and together these stories represent a broad spectrum of American history. In each story, there is an obvious desire to truly honor the men who fulfilled the role of father in unforgettable ways. Get out your hankies and crank up the laugh machine, we've got heartbreakers and laughmakers. And, in the end, should you feel inspired, write a letter to your dad, gift him with this delightful book, and encourage him to nestle down with these stories—he'll thank you for it.

And to all fathers everywhere, thank you!

In My Father's Truck

LAURA PRITCHETT

. . . is an extra pipe, orange bailing twine, a tape of cowboy poet Baxter Black, a bottle of Gink ("World's Best Dry Fly Dressing"), a black film canister full of fishing flies (bought for a buck each from his barber), Dr. Grabow pipe filters, an "Emeritus" parking permit for the university, and a Stetson cowboy hat size 59-7⅜. There is the ever-present bottle of mouthwash to erase the smell of pipe smoke from his breath, which he does for my mother's benefit, which irritates more than appeases her because then, she says, he smells like tobacco covered in mint. There is a pair of sunglasses that has apparently been stepped on, because the frame is tilted sideways. There's lots of dust and bits of hay.

My father is standing in the Yampa River in northern Colorado. He doesn't like dry fly fishing, though he can do it. Instead he casts upstream, lets the fly sink a little as it drifts down, and just as the fly starts to turn back, he reels it in. He takes a puff from his pipe, casts again, pauses once to change flies.

I've been in Steamboat for a few days, by myself, and I'm staying in the old hunting cabin he built about the same time I was born. The place is falling apart, but it's my favorite place to go. The town of Steamboat Springs spreads in one direction, and Emerald Mountain rises to the other, and mainly I find it beautiful because it reminds me of him.

My father looks so happy now, and he often says that he is. This is how he always describes himself: *just a happy guy.* Other people tell me this too: "Your father is the nicest man! So kind and gentle, so quiet, so calm, so considerate, so friendly."

I shrug and say, "Well, I know. He is." He lets things pass over him, like water—the best example of meditation practice I have, though he knows nothing about the formal practice of meditation. It's just that he believes life comes with pain and since he expects it, it doesn't crush him; and he believes life comes with joy, and so it doesn't fluster him. I need to remember to be like him, especially at moments like this, when I am afraid this will be the *last, best* we'll have together. He's getting older; I'm getting busier; when else are we going to find ourselves alone by a mountain stream?

I get out of the truck and walk out next to him. I'm not in the mood to fish, so I sit on the beach and sift pebbles through my fingers. Dad is smoking his pipe, an old corncob thing, out of fashion but his favorite, and he always smokes Middleton's Cherry Blend tobacco, a red and white package I have known from earliest memory. Sometimes for gifts I get him fancier versions of cherry-blend tobacco, but he always likes cheap Middleton's the best..He's wearing a bright turquoise Western shirt and Wranglers and has, temporarily, changed from his cowboy boots to brown hip waders. His hair is all white now, as are the unshaved whiskers poking from his red-tough skin.

"Had one a while ago," he says. "Hook didn't set."

His line periodically wisps above me; every so often it gets close enough that I duck. I could move, I guess, but I'm settled into this sunny spot that's mottled in soft colors of smooth pebbles. It is evening, so this circle of sun has captured me and protected me from the chill.

My father is mumbling too about the drought, the low levels of water, the huge wildfire to our south that makes the air smell like a campfire. He's talking about his life as a rancher and a university professor, about how they both suited him just fine. He's mumbling about his childhood, my childhood, and the future.

I like watching him mumble. He talks in half-sentences, like I do, perhaps because we both feel awkward taking up more space and noise than we need to. Or perhaps it's because he's simply trying to fish, which takes up most of his concentration.

Though I am sitting quietly, he says to me now, "Laura, you're a force to be reckoned with."

This is his famous line to describe me. It was the one and only contribution to my baby book: *Kid, you're a force to be reckoned with*, and he still likes this image of me as fierce and stubborn and independent. I think that now it's his way of telling me loves me, though he does that, too—uses those words, "Love ya", he says—but this speaks more to something particular in me, whether it is real or imagined, that he finds amusing and admirable.

So we have talked a little, but this is what I like best: watching him.

"I can rig up a pole," my father says now. "You want me to rig up a pole?"

"No, I'll just watch," I say. I think, *I could rig up my own pole; you taught me how.* I find it funny that he keeps offering to do the things he's already taught me.

He casts again. He watches the river. I watch him.

"Hey! Hey there, hey!" He's got one. He reels it in, crouches to take it off, a puff of pipe smoke fills the air, and then the rainbow trout, flapping its tail furiously, is held in his hands. Then it's slipping away, back into the water, as he releases it to be free. "Hot dog," he says. "That was a pretty one."

"It sure was," I say. And I mean: This moment with you is shimmering and beautiful.

LAURA PRITCHETT is the author of a novel, *Sky Bridge* (winner of the WILLA Literary Award; finalist for the Dublin International Award and the Colorado Book Award) and a collection of short stories, *Hell's Bottom, Colorado* (winner of the PEN USA award and the Milkweed National Fiction Prize). Pritchett is coeditor and contributor to two books: *Home Land: Ranching and a West That Works* and *The Pulse of the River: Colorado Writers Speak for the Endangered Cache la Poudre.* Her newest book is a memoir about her ranching family.

Driving Toward Yes

DAWN DOWNEY

In the summer of 1964, Dad stood at the edge of the Mojave Desert. With his three teenagers, he watched the family cat give birth in the back of the station wagon. The hot wind whispered *yes* as it blew across his brow. Five days earlier, at age forty-three, he closed up Bill's Body Shop, his car repair business. He waved goodbye to relatives and friends. He drove away from Des Moines, leading a four-vehicle caravan down Route 66. He was off to California in pursuit of dreams.

Only a high school graduate himself, Dad insisted that his kids would go to college. He had five, number six on the way, and no means to finance all that education. But he'd read that the University of California was tuition-free for the state's residents. The fact that no job awaited him in the Golden State—he'd work that out later. Dad said *yes* to his dreams, when logic warned *not so fast*.

He drove the station wagon and pulled a U-Haul trailer. My eighteen-year-old sister Michelle, who'd earned her driver's license two weeks before, drove a second car. She towed a yellow VW Beetle that Dad planned to sell when we got to California. Besides Cass, our calico cat, two other passengers rode along— my twelve-year-old brother Bill and me, age fourteen.

My older brother stayed behind to complete his degree at the local community college. Our pregnant mother and year-old baby brother had flown out ahead of us, and awaited our arrival at the home of Dad's best friend in Pasadena.

A water pump or two broke along the way. An eighteen-wheeler mangled the trailer hitch. And Dad and Michelle parted company for a while—he following the arrow on a detour sign, she driving around the sign and heading toward Canada. But the four of us ended up together at the edge of the Mojave. While waiting to cross it in the cool of the night, we watched Cass birth her kittens while the sun painted the sky pale pink, then navy blue. Michelle, Bill, and I gawked at the foreign landscape, fussed over the cat and complained about the heat. Dad towered over us, as big as the desert.

Early the next morning he delivered his brood—three kids and five cats—to Pasadena. (The kids went on to college; the cats did not.)

Long before our cross-country trek, my father had outgrown his life in Des Moines. Between pounding out fenders, he'd written his first novel, in longhand on a green legal pad. A year after the move to California, the *Santa Barbara News Press* hired him on the strength of an article he'd submitted. He was their first African American reporter. He walked into the interview straight from his job as a mechanic at the local Ford dealership. His muscled six-foot frame stuffed into a pair of blue coveralls, he navigated a twilight zone between laborer and wordsmith. Something told him he could write and the force of the dream propelled him.

While working at the paper, he typed his second novel during lunch breaks, in the back of his camper.

He stretched the newspaper job from obituary writer into outdoor columnist. Every week, he expanded "Gone Fishin'" beyond the expected descriptions of the best camping spots and the latest model boats. His readers got to know his old Uncle Russell in Ottumwa, and his brother the TV weatherman in Des Moines, as well as his wife the poet. When Uncle Russell got sick, he received hundreds of get-well cards from all across the country. I suspected then that Dad might be more than just the guy who grounded me.

After a ten-year stint as newspaper columnist, he outgrew that life too. He transformed himself into freelance writer and then again into published author, with five books to his credit.

Dad kept growing, busting out the seams of every life he wore. He supplemented his income by teaching memoir writing through adult education. And that's how he became a guru, the only career big enough to fit. Others taught; Dad cheered, encouraged, cajoled, nudged, wept, nagged, poked, and charmed. He mesmerized his students toward their dreams. One described the classroom experience as a cross between a quilting bee and a revival meeting.

Dad's bass voice boomed, but he critiqued his novice writers as gently as he held his grandbabies. "You're safe here," he whispered to a trembling woman before she read her story out loud.

Ladies flocked around him before class. Men lingered afterward. Repeaters were common. Many took his course five years in a row. One returned fifteen times. On the rare occasions that illness kept him home, Dad learned that his substitutes were greeted with surly expressions and sarcastic complaints. My father had groupies.

He taught for thirty years and liked to tell the story about the day he realized just how long that was. At the beginning of one semester, a young woman approached him, her hair swishing as she walked. He straightened himself and puffed his chest. "Mr. Downey, I'm so excited to be in your class," she said. "My grandmother took it ten years ago and she just loved you." Dad laughed the loudest at jokes on himself.

He told his students to take more risks and write to their edge. That's how he lived. That's what he expected.

When I was twenty-eight, home for the holidays, my teenaged sister and I were feuding. She swept past me to greet other family members with effusive air kisses. Wherever she stood she turned her back to me. I confided to Dad that I'd rather spend Christmas with friends, than endure her silent treatment. It had reduced me from career woman to schoolyard victim. As the scent of pine and cinnamon embraced us, he wrapped me in a Daddy bear hug, and then encouraged me to stay and work it out. "You can't quit. I don't call you Snake Bite for nothing."

That was the only time he'd ever called me Snake Bite. But I stayed and worked it out. I took the risk because he knew I could do it.

Decades after his death, Dad still tells me that I can do it. When alien landscapes stretch ahead, he towers over me, big as the desert. Through divorce, layoffs, and career changes, he challenges me to take a risk. When I'm typing against a deadline in the middle of the night, I catch sight of him standing at the edge of the Mojave. And I remember Dad driving toward *yes*. ✺

DAWN DOWNEY has had essays published by *The Christian Science Monitor*, *Skirt! Magazine*, *The Best Times*, and *Kansas City Voices Magazine*. Her work earned first prize for creative nonfiction at the 2005 Santa Barbara Writers Conference, where 200 of her dad's former students cheered her on. Two other essays earned first and second prizes in the Missouri Writers Guild 2007 Winter Writing Contest.

God Almighty, Damn!

RAMON CARVER

People take high school or college diplomas for granted, *unless they never got one.* My mother and father never graduated from high school; so my dad giggled like a kid at my high school graduation ceremony. He also shook my hand and told me he was very proud of me.

And then, not long after, my dad suffered a stroke and couldn't say much about anything. But he never viewed himself as sick; he would only accept one descriptive term: incapacitated. And he lived another twenty-five years, a very angry man at first, until he resigned himself to having only three words that he could say with any spontaneity—in a row—and those words were: "God Almighty, Damn!"

Mother was always a bit chagrined, "I wish he wouldn't say that! Nobody should take the Lord's name in vain. But," she said, "that's all the poor man can say."

No, it wasn't, actually. He could say, "Yes" or "Okay," or "Pretty day!" or "Pretty day, okay?" Or when he got excited or confused, he'd say, "Pretty day, God Almighty, Damn!"

The day I graduated from college, after we returned home from the graduation ceremony, I handed Dad my diploma, and said, "This is a return on your investment in my education."

Dad studied it and said, "Pretty day," and then he tried to say—I am *sure* he tried to say—"I am mighty proud of you, son," but he stopped after several attempts to form the words, put the diploma down, and turned away, as if embarrassed.

I remember feeling cheated on two counts because I longed to hear him express how proud he was that I had graduated from Yale, but I didn't want to make it obvious how much I wanted to make him proud. I didn't want to sound sentimental *and* stupid. And I didn't want to embarrass him either.

My dad wasn't ever helpless, and he didn't want pity. There were just some things he couldn't do very well. Like walk straight and talk. And he had always been right-handed, but he was never able to use his right hand after the stroke, only his left hand, which he took to calling "it." "It" gave him fits. "It" did everything all wrong—not him, *it!* Then he'd laugh at himself.

He had a great, robust laugh. He never lost that.

Dad was always doing things Mom didn't want him doing, and vice versa, really. They lived in Tampa, in a stucco house, and it drove Mom crazy that Dad insisted on painting the outside of the house—every other year! Don't ask why. I don't know, because he never tried to explain. He just said he was going to do it, and—God Almighty, Damn!—he did it. "It" would take about two years to finish—and then Dad would start again. He was proud of his handiwork and would call me on the day he finally laid his brush down and expect me to understand what he meant when he'd say, "Pretty day!"

Mom also didn't want him using the phone: "He gets everything so dirty. He smeared stucco paint on the buffet! All over the sidewalk! On the azaleas!"

But whenever Mom left the house, if the phone rang, Dad would run for it, crashing into the desk, grabbing the phone, and answering, "Yes!" Sometimes he'd take notes that none of us could read. And that's what happened the day after my college graduation.

I had gone on an errand with my mother, so Dad was home alone when the phone rang. Like always, he snapped it up, and answered, "Yes!" It was a friend calling for me, so Dad picked up a pencil and painstakingly wrote down. Each. Number. Slowly. Laboriously. Using "it."

Then, he hung up the phone and discovered he had used the backside of my diploma for scratch paper.

So he tried to erase it, and the more he erased, the more he smeared the face of the diploma. When we came through the door, he was still standing beside the phone in an obvious state of shock.

I knew something was wrong, but he wouldn't look at me.

Finally, he held up the diploma and muttered, "God Almighty, Damn!" And then quietly, "Okay?"

Thank goodness I had the presence of mind to reassure Dad that it didn't matter. "Really, Dad! After all, until now it was just another diploma, but now—and forever—it'll be mine and yours!"

My dad looked like a little boy, baffled at first, and then slowly comprehending what I was saying. Finally, he smiled, his face beaming, clearly pleased with the solution. It would be *our* diploma.

The next day, I took the smeared diploma to a frame shop, and told them it was fine to frame it the way it was. You can't tell it's smudged and dirty—if you stand about five feet away.

After all, a college diploma is one of those mementos we hang on walls and barely notice. But now mine is special. Every time I look at my diploma, it's that same afternoon, and I see my Dad with that little boy smile on his face. God Almighty, Damn. Pretty day!

RAMON CARVER, cursed with the name of a great short story writer, is the author of plays produced professionally from New York to L.A. He was recently profiled as one of fifty *Hometown Heroes: Real Stories of Ordinary People Doing Extraordinary Things*, on www.HarperCollins.com and one of his essays appeared in *My Teacher Is My Hero*. View more of his work on *www.ramoncarver.com*.

Carry On, Dad

ANDREW McALEER

In my first novel *Appearance of Counsel*, I wanted to introduce a secondary character who had served in World War II, a quiet and unassuming person who had experienced firsthand pain, death, and ruin, yet remained an individual who could find a way to use the atrocities of war for the betterment of others—someone like my father, John McAleer.

My father served as a medic in World War II. When a young GI of Mexican descent received burns on over two-thirds of his body, my father nursed him for over six months. During that time, my father learned that the soldier's brother had died in Anzio, and that he was his mother's last remaining child. When the young soldier succumbed to his injuries, my father wrote a personal letter to the soldier's mother to explain what happened, so that she wouldn't receive a generic form letter telling her that her last remaining son had also died. Decades later, my father couldn't remember the soldier's name, but thought of him as personally representative of all the "unknown soldiers" who died fighting for freedom.

Because he was never one to boast or brag, my father didn't tell me this story, or any others about his experiences in World War II, until I was fully grown. I remember feeling proud of his heroism and realizing for the first time that my father had witnessed the most horrific results of war. It was obvious that he still mourned the soldier and still worried about how his mother had coped with her losses. What impressed me most was knowing how many young men my father had watched return home—without limbs, or sight, or with a permanently severed spirit—and realizing that my father found ways to cope and to grow despite his experiences.

When my father returned home from the war, he completed college and earned a PhD in English from Harvard. He taught at Harvard and then Boston College for more than half a century; he also published fifteen books, including his biography on Ralph Waldo Emerson, which was nominated for a Pulitzer Prize. But as remarkable as my father's academic and literary career was, these were not his finest accomplishments.

My father maintained a passion for the little things in life. Through actions more than words he taught me to love books and literature, but also to appreciate gardening, woodworking, and my next meal. He also taught me life skills, like how to save money and avoid waste. He modeled generosity and compassion, strongly extolling the virtue of valuing the anonymous workers who make the best effort they can to contribute. He didn't consider it enough to offer compassion for the less fortunate; he always offered genuine encouragement as well.

The people my father most admired were the ones out there working the day-to-day grind. As an eclectic scholar, he would often find himself lecturing on Thoreau, Austen, Dreiser, or even Sherlock Holmes, but the people he felt most comfortable with were the guy who could make an engine run; the woman who could frame a picture; the octogenarian Irishman at the church who kept the lawn so green; people who took pride in the seemingly insignificant task ahead. Most of all he admired my mother, Ruth, who managed to teach high school full time, raise six children, *and* carry stove-hot dishes to the table bare handed.

About ten years before my father passed away he was diagnosed with cancer. Naturally, he continued to write and teach until his death. A day or two after he passed away, his oncologist told me that my father used to forgo treatment until the end of each semester so it wouldn't interfere with his teaching.

Not too long ago I showed my eight-year-old nephew, Liam, my father's World War II uniform. Like everyone, he felt awed by my father's courage so I let him slip on the jacket. He wanted to know where his grandfather had fought, and I gently reminded him that his grandfather was a medic who fought to save lives, not take them. I told him his grandfather always believed that the best weapon a soldier can have is his mind, and that it was the only weapon he employed to fight the enemy. I told Liam that it is our job now to realize the dream of freedom the soldiers like his grandfather held so dear.

I sometimes marvel at how many students my father taught over the years—students who are now making law, doctoring the sick, working for peace, writing novels, and taking their kids to the latest museum exhibit. Was the spirit of that unknown soldier with him every step of the way? Knowing my father, I think he was. And when I see admiration for his grandfather alive in Liam's eyes, I'd say he still is.

Carry on, Dad. You're doing a good job.

ANDREW McALEER works for the Massachusetts Department of Corrections. He coauthored the number-one best-seller *Mystery Writing in a Nutshell*, and recently authored *101 Habits of Highly Successful Novelists*. Mr. McAleer is also a Specialist with the Army National Guard.

The Exalted Big Dipper of Chicago, Illinois, USA

JAN HENRIKSON

"Sliced jelly is my own invention. It may sweep the world," announced Dad in a breathless voice. He didn't mean it, of course. He was reading the part of Victor Gook, a character from his favorite radio comedy.

My little sister and I squished our small bodies next to him on our plastic-wrapped couch. We held the Script Book on our laps like a hymnal, stifling giggles as we read our lines and made the appropriate sound effects.

Chortles. Sighs. Coughs. Sounding off was almost as much fun as running through the playground of words before us. Hanging upside down on one phrase, swinging on another. I'd never heard such language.

Take Rush, the son in this radio comedy. He never sits on the couch. He is "gelatinously athwart the davenport." He doesn't just read. He "somewhat sluggishly glances through a volume of vigorous fiction."

"That poor cast," said Dad. He would shake his head, marveling at *Vic and Sade's* quirky fifteen-minute dialogues, the ones he and his Mom listened to faithfully for nearly ten years when he was growing up. "They had to bite their tongues to keep from cracking up. Sometimes you'd hear them laughing on air."

Who'd ever dream that a radio show cooked up in the early 1930s could possibly tickle two little girls in the late '60s? Dad, that's who.

To Dad, creativity was king. He savored the sweet oddities of daily life as if they were rare delicacies. He offered them to his daughters for savoring, too.

That's what I like to think, anyway.

Perhaps he reached for these plays as a last resort. A way to distract us from our sisterly fights which entailed a lot of Red-Faced Pinching, followed by Fake Crying and Name-Calling.

All I know is we were hooked. We had to have our *Vic and Sade*. Once a week, we turned our backs on Ping-Pong championships and card games and landed headfirst into their "small house halfway up the block."

How could we not be fascinated by Victor Gook, Exalted Big Dipper of the Drowsy Venus Chapter of the Sacred Stars of the Milky Way Fraternal Order? Or his friend, Rishigan Fishigan of Sishigan, Michigan?

Forget the characters. What about their adventures? In one episode Vic and son Rush delight in giving each other an escalating series of electrical jolts while attempting to fix Sade's washing machine. In another, Rush "drums up a little excitement" on a summer's day by rolling rocks into caramels on the hot sidewalk.

Riveting stuff to our grade school minds. And not unlike our own whimsies.

Dad encouraged us to concoct our own stories and skits. To twirl while he played the piano, all the while wondering about the universe and who thought it up. Why stars? What if they were making wishes on us? Imagination was not fluff to us. Not the mere jovial sidekick to practicality. It was the force that ran the world.

"You know Paul Rhymer wrote an episode every morning for that day's show. Can you believe that?" asked Dad. "For the love of Pete!"

I could believe that. When Dad was not re-enacting *Vic and Sade* with us, he was playing the role of cartoonist. Professional editorial cartoonist, that is. He had deadlines every day too. To my young mind, it seemed he woke up every morning with nothing but pencil doodles on a piece of paper. And at night, *voilà!* he rushed to the local airport just in the nick of time. There, a small, loud plane (which I vowed to learn how to fly someday) soared away with his finished cartoon. All this excitement just so a newspaper in a far-off city could publish his cartoon in their next edition.

His cartoons were proof! Just because you couldn't see something—yet—didn't mean it didn't exist.

"Just think," Dad would enthuse, "ideas are all around us, waiting for the person who's paying attention. They're like radio waves, broadcasting through the air all the time. They're right here where you're standing! Why do you think people who live on different sides of the world, people who've never heard of each other, invent the same things at the same time?"

That meant that this cast of characters—Vic and Sade and Rush—and their friends, Smelly Clark and Blue-Tooth Johnson, and let's not forget Ike Kneesuffer who plays indoor horseshoes in his basement—that means that all of them had been hanging around the ether, waiting for someone to go "Aha!"

These characters would have slapped my Dad on the back and given him a gooseberry pie just for twirling his eyebrows when he was tired. They would have admired the way he always kept a pencil behind his ear and a sketchpad in his pocket, on the look-out for peculiar facial features.

Like me, they would have missed him every time he went on the road to give his Chalk Talks, otherwise titled, "Cartooning Is a Funny Business." There, he drew caricatures of the audience and made quips about the cartooning process.

In the early days, he tried to grip his huge pad of paper on his knee like a ventriloquist's dummy.

Finally, a cousin said, "Hey, why don't you get an easel?"

"It made it a lot easier," said Dad, laughing at himself.

I'm convinced. If Dad didn't already exist, Paul Rhymer would have surely invented him. It would have been his best idea since sliced jelly.

JAN HENRIKSON thanks the Muses for creating her dad. A writer, editor, and writing coach, she has been published in many anthologies, including *Chicken Soup for the Dieter's Soul*, and *A Cup of Comfort® for Writers*. She is editor of *Eat by Choice, Not by Habit* (Puddle Dancer Press, 2005). When in doubt, Jan chooses chocolate.

The Woodworker's Song

ROXANNE WERNER

After saving for several years, my husband and I owned a plot of land, a set of blueprints, and a construction mortgage. Now the large hole dug for my house's foundation gaped at my feet threatening to swallow us—and our plans. Staring into the muddy hole, I felt overwhelmed by the prospect of building a house from scratch. The blueprints meant nothing to me. They might as well have been written in another language. The bank's deadlines loomed large. Worries and doubts filled my mind. The high-pitched whine of an electric saw split the air. Plywood fell with a crash like wooden cymbals and snapped me out of my gloomy thoughts. Birds flew up screeching in alarm; squirrels and rabbits scurried for cover. The noise frightened them, but not me. Those sounds had run through my life as long as I could remember. It was my father's music, the woodworker's song.

Suddenly I was little again tromping down the steps to my father's cellar workroom. Lured by the siren's call of the electric saw, my footsteps echoed on the wooden treads. I sat on a stool mesmerized by the blur of the blade's spinning teeth. Clouds of sawdust swirled like snowflakes and came to rest in fluffy drifts beneath the table. The spicy aroma of wood sap mixed with the faint burning smell from the saw's friction.

My father was a carpenter. I spent hours watching him create things while I played with wood shavings that stretched and snapped back like the curls in my hair. His fair arms were burnt a permanent bronze by years of working outdoors. His clothes were speckled with sawdust or paint. His workshop held a tool for just about everything. No job was too big or too small. He could switch easily from shingling the roof to building a dollhouse. Once he even drilled holes through hundreds of seeds because I wanted to string them as a necklace. Every day around supper I would hear him whistling in the driveway and know he was home. His whistle seemed to continue the song he played all day on his tools; the singing of a saw, the pounding beat of a hammer.

The memories flooded my heart and yanked me back from the hole before my feet. I turned to see my father already busy at work. All the things I watched him make in our cellar were just a part of his trade; a table, a bookshelf, and a cabinet were small tasks to tune up his tools. I never saw him at his real work of building houses. He spent a lifetime building homes for others. Now his talents were put to use building one for me. He read the blueprints as a maestro reads a musical score and conducted the song that was to become my home.

In the weeks that followed my husband and I learned to know our house inside out. Under my father's direction a wooden skeleton rose from the foundation.

"Bring those two-by-fours over here," my father called. "And how about a cup of coffee?"

His powerful arms banged nails in with one or two sure strokes. Nails jingled in the canvas pouch around his waist as he reached for more. My own hammering was a light staccato tapping. It took me at least ten taps to drive in a nail.

"Darn," I said as I bent another nail. My father reached over and yanked it out with the hammer's claw. He pounded a new one in with one stroke and gave me a wink.

"Don't be so timid," he said. "You won't hurt the nails."

I soon got the hang of it and was driving nails into the house's plywood skin while singing Gordon Lightfoot's "Canadian Railroad Trilogy." My father's music flowed through me.

The shell of the house went up quickly. But then things slowed to a crawl. It was surprising how many details went into a finished house. My father led us through layer upon layer. Each needed to be done before moving on to the next. An electrician ran wires. A plumber put in pipes. We stuffed the walls with pink cotton candy insulation. Sheetrock was hung and spackled. The list of things went on and on.

We all worked regular jobs. Yet we still had to meet the bank's deadlines. My father gave up his vacations, weekends, and evenings to help us. All our spare time went into it. But there were no shortcuts allowed. Everything had to have my father's seal of approval. I remember varnishing our doors and trim over and over again.

"Dad, I'm sure developers don't put eight coats of varnish on these things," I said.

"Maybe they don't. But I'm not a developer. I'm a carpenter," he said. "You should give them one more coat."

I rolled my eyes. But I gave them the extra coat of varnish. I knew this house was his gift to me. If my father had been a writer, he would have written me a poem; if a musician, a song. But his talent was to build things and my house was his masterwork.

We've lived many years in the house my father built. The mortgage is paid. We've watched our son grow up here. We've celebrated birthdays and holidays. The walls have echoed with our laughter and our tears. The house he built turned into a noisy home. Still sometimes when it's quiet, I run my hands over a door. I feel the smooth wood and I remember the summer my father taught us to play the woodworker's song.

ROXANNE WERNER lives and writes in the house her father built with her husband, son, and two cats. If you would like to read more of her work, her story "Indomitable Spirit" is part of the *My Teacher Is My Hero* anthology.

Pop, the Unpretentious Guru

JIM SCHIELDGE

One of my earliest childhood memories is watching my dad trudging through deep snow on his way to work as a mail carrier in East Hartford, Connecticut. A blizzard was raging in the middle of the harsh winter of 1943. I watched wide-eyed from my warm perch in the living room window of our modest house as this figure I idolized, a shadow against the swirling New England snow, slowly disappeared as if swallowed by an enveloping white blanket. I felt that if he came back from that terrible force, he was surely invincible and would live forever. Of course he did come back, again and again. We needed him, and his devotion to our family never wavered.

Philip Adam Schieldge was the quintessential nice guy, soft-spoken and unassuming, almost to a fault. He was an old-fashioned man, with an old-fashioned name, who married the only love in his life, his sweetheart, Henrietta. He had a kind word or a warm pat on the shoulder for everyone. In all the years

I knew him, I never heard him utter a single profanity. He wasn't a religious man, but he certainly was a moral man. I never saw him turn his head to look at a pretty girl. It wasn't that he was a prude, not by any means; it's just that the idea of looking at another woman was completely foreign to him. After all, he was a married man, and married men didn't do that. The people on his mail route appreciated him too. He would come home with little packages that smelled wonderful, full of meats and sauces from his patrons in the Italian neighborhood or barbecued ribs from his African American friends who wanted to share with this quiet, friendly mailman.

The postal tribute chiseled in stone at the Smithsonian's Postal Museum reads, "Neither rain, nor sleet, nor gloom of night stays these couriers from the swift completion of their appointed rounds." Dad embodied this dedication until one especially bad winter forced him to a decision. He sat us down at the dinner table and, with a twinkle in his eye, asked, "Who wants to move to California?" We three children were all for it. California! The Wild West! Cowboys, Indians, movie stars! Mom, however, was skeptical. All of her family and friends lived in Connecticut. World War II was raging, and things were unsettled all over the country. Dad promised us a better life, though, and soon we boarded the train west, chugging off to an uncertain future.

The post office wasn't hiring full-time help then, so Dad rolled up his sleeves and found work at the Long Beach Naval Shipyards. His patriotism compelled him to contribute to the war effort as well as provide for us. In his off-hours, he worked part-time at the post office. He wanted to prove to Mom that he had made a good financial decision. His hard work paid off, and the post office soon hired him on as a full-time employee. He quit his shipyard job and didn't tell us until years later how dangerous it was walking home from the docks at night or that he had been brutally mugged one night. Neither rain, nor sleet, nor gloom of night, nor thugs were going to prevent him from fulfilling his responsibilities to his family.

Once he was settled at the post office, Dad concentrated on raising his family and pursuing his hobby of following horse racing at Santa Anita Park in Arcadia. Appropriate for him, his name Philip means "lover of horses." He would drive to the track, wear his lucky straw hat with the brim turned up all around, and confidently wager his two-dollar bets. He never wanted to bet more and possibly lose enough to tip off Mom that he was short of money. His favorite expression became, "I could've made a bundle. I knew that horse was going to win." He gave out more tips than a Damon Runyon tout. His grateful recipients at the track always did well and often pulled in lucrative returns. Dad's payoff consisted of helping others, not in lining his own pocket. He taught me to never pass up an opportunity to help someone, no matter how small the gesture. As we kids aged, our appreciation of his quiet strength and his teaching us life lessons by example grew, and we took to calling him the affectionate term, Pop, instead of Dad. He never objected.

When Mom developed Alzheimer's disease late in life, Pop's devotion to her never lessened. He read articles to her from the morning paper while she rocked in her chair, smiling and nodding. Whether she understood or not was beside the point. His patience with her during this difficult time matched that of a saint. When her condition deteriorated to the point that he couldn't care for her at home anymore, I witnessed their last moment together on the little porch of their bungalow as she left to start life anew in a care facility. Pop kissed her face gently and said, "Goodbye, Hen." With sad eyes he watched his wife of sixty-one years walk down the front path and out of his life. They never spent another night together.

When I would visit him later at his home alone, I would look into his face and see this wonderful man, Pop, the giant who had lifted me as a child and tossed me in the air as I squealed with delight. I would remember his lessons that taught me kindness and humor and racial tolerance before it became fashionable. Fragments of memories would swirl around us just like the snowflakes that were whipped by that New England wind so long ago. I would look into his soft, blue eyes and recognize anew that familiar, quiet strength and draw from it. That's when I would tell myself, I am truly in the presence of a hero, my Dad, my Pop.

JIM SCHIELDGE is a retired fire battalion chief who emulates his father's example of helping others. He currently trains staffs in nursing homes and convalescent hospitals in fire and disaster procedures. Jim was a featured columnist in his city hall newspaper and is currently writing a novel based on his years of firefighting experiences.

That Silver-Haired Daddy of Mine

PAULA MUNIER

My father is a sophisticated man. He speaks several languages, has lived on several continents, and has traveled all over the world. He's led many lives: military officer, financier, even diplomat. But to hear him tell it, he's just a farm boy who made good. It's a claim he always makes whenever he sniffs even a hint of snobbery/ego/impertinence on my part.

"I'm just a hick from Perry County," he says. "You come from a long line of hicks. And don't you forget it."

This "hick" persona is one he pulls out whenever he finds himself in the company of elitists. Much like the "hired killer" role he assumes for any military-bashing civilians he may encounter, his hick character nearly always fools the, well, fools. He lays it on thick; in a suddenly trilling Midwestern twang, he'll launch into a long, bumbling hymn to hound dogs, rabbit stew, and country/western music. He'll even sing, usually something by his favorite guitar-slinging cowboy, Gene Autry. "Red River Valley." "Tumblin' Tumbleweeds." "Back in the Saddle Again."

Now that country is cool, this last ploy sometimes backfires. All manner of snobs now profess to be fans of the musical genre once reserved exclusively for the *Hee Haw* crowd. You can imagine what Dad thinks of these latte-drinking, BMW-driving upstarts. I once took him to a Garth Brooks concert at the convention center in Las Vegas, where he denounced the ratio of foreign cars to pickups in the parking lot. "Who are all these people? Why aren't they over at the Hilton lining up for Barry Manilow?" Still, Dad enjoyed the concert, even though he grumbled afterward that Garth was "no Gene Autry."

When I was a kid, I'd sing along with my dad to the radio. There was no newfangled crossover country back then; it was all Hank Williams and Ernest Tubbs and the ubiquitous Gene Autry. We got a kick out of the silliest lyrics—the cornier the better—and the sorriest narratives—the more pitiful, the better. Our favorite sing-alongs: Roy Clark and "Thank God and Greyhound She's Gone." Johnny Cash and "A Boy Named Sue." Eric Heatherly and "Countin' Flowers on the Wall."

I can see now that the writer in me was born somewhere on the back roads of Indiana, driving around with Dad and listening to these sad, ironic stories masquerading as ditties. I'm grateful to him for it, but I'm not sure he would tell you he'd done a good thing there.

It's not that Dad doesn't like writers or writing. He likes a good Louis L'Amour story as much as the next guy. Dad's own father was a schoolteacher, who valued fine storytelling above all else. My grandfather was a lively character, always quick with a story but sometimes slow to honor his familial obligations. He taught Dad to love stories, even as he might distrust storytellers. Dad would grow up to become everything his father was not: a man who put family, God, and country before all else. A man who could fix your car and train your dog and take in your wayward teenagers. A man who could jump out of airplanes and handle any manner of weaponry and save your ass in combat. A man who might spin you a good yarn, but would also protect you from all enemies, including yourself.

Still, as a good son Dad passed on the best part of his father's legacy to his only child. When I was a kid, whenever I cried Dad would cheer me up with Grandpa's favorite aphorism: "It doesn't matter what happens to you, little girl, as long as it makes a good story later."

Of course, Dad doesn't tell me that any more; he doesn't want to encourage me. I've written a lot about my dad and his heroic exploits—and a lot of what I've written has been published. Often to his chagrin.

"She makes it all up," he tells people who ask him about my writing. "Those things never really happened."

Poor Dad. As much as he loves me, I know I am at times an embarrassment to him. In this way and many others I am much like my grandfather. I laugh too loud and too much. I'm a terrible driver. I have trouble staying married. I can be *way* too full of myself.

And I believe in turning bad luck into good stories.

Which is, after all, what country music is all about. And whether he likes it or not, I have my father to thank for that. He introduced me to country music. In the age of Elvis and the Beatles, he turned me on to Hank and Ernest and Gene. (Did I tell you about the time Dad met Elvis? Elvis was a G.I. in Germany, and helped my dad pull a jeep out of the mud. "Good soldier," was my father's singular comment about this momentous event.)

Even now, when my iPod's loaded with everything from Mozart to Maroon 5, I still turn to country when I need inspiration. Feminist that I am, I've added girl singers to Dad's repertoire of real men: Patsy, Dolly, Mary Chapin Carpenter. But my all-time favorite country song remains the one that reminds me most of my father, the classic written by his pals Gene Autry and Jimmy Long, "That Silver-Haired Daddy of Mine." In this solid-gold tearjerker, the singing cowboy laments the cares and woes he has visited upon his father, and wishes he could take back everything he ever did to worry dear old dad.

As a parent now myself, I understand how great that worry can be. I also understand that the hardest things to give your kids are the only things that really matter: a strong sense of self and a good character. For these they learn only by example—yours, good and bad. For these I had the very best teacher, my dad. From him I learned to be true to myself as a writer and as a woman. And whenever I got a little too big for my britches, he was there to set me straight. He still does. The good news is that the older I get, the less I need it. As a young woman, I was desperate to be considered urbane, intellectual, worldly. I've spent the last fifty years adding layer after layer of sophistication to my persona, only to realize that my father had it right all along.

It's fine to be sophisticated in the ways of the world, as long as you're homely in the ways of the soul.

Now I'm proud to say that I'm a hick at heart.

Just like Dad. ❧

PAULA MUNIER is Director of Innovation for Adams Media. She is also president of the New England Chapter of Mystery Writers of America. Her stories and essays have appeared in numerous anthologies. She successfully raised two children and currently lives on the South Shore in Massachusetts, with her son Mikey, two dogs, and a cat.

Of Pigs and Wren

CAROL E. AYER

That summer Dad and I had a nickname for everything, most of them irreverent. We were vacationing in England at the time, and British names seemed to lend themselves to being made fun of. The Wig and Pen, a classic English pub in Covent Garden, became "The Pig and Wren." Thorpe Park, the amusement park we found vastly inferior to Disneyland, became "Warped Park." And we decided on "Flibberty" for Liberty, the upscale shop in London's fashionable Regent Street. Of course, each member of the family had to have a nickname as well. My stepmother, Susan, was now Suzie Q; my baby half-sister, Michelle, was My Belle; and Dad and I formed the comedy team of Bigs and Pigs.

The playfulness that brought about these nicknames reflected our mood at the time. After many years of unease between us, my father and I were finally getting along. When I was young, he worked a lot and wasn't around for my swim meets or school functions. I always felt he didn't care about me very much. He was quick to criticize and to punish. When he and my mother divorced, I blamed him for the breakup.

Then, within a few years, Dad and my mom each remarried. While at first I was wary of the changes, I eventually came to accept the new family structure and the new routines. I lived with my mother and stepfather during the week, and visited my dad and his family on weekends.

I was also lucky enough to spend vacations in London, where Dad and Susan owned a flat just minutes from Parliament and Westminster Abbey. This particular summer, I was in my early twenties and enjoying every moment of my British vacation. I'd caught a glimpse of Charles and Diana leaving Kensington Palace, I'd spent hours poring over original manuscripts at the British Museum, and I'd drooled over the treats in the Food Hall at Harrod's. During the day we traveled around the countryside, and at night we went out on the town to restaurants and plays and musicals. It was an easy, luxurious life.

Best of all, my dad and I were closer than we'd ever been. We played countless hours of tennis, each trying to outdo the other, and followed Wimbledon religiously. The father I remembered was serious and stern, stressed from too much work and an unhappy marriage. But this dad was fun and spontaneous. Clearly, he had made peace with the past and was enjoying life with his new family. He was careful to keep me in the thick of things, always introducing me as "the oldest daughter" so I wouldn't feel left out. I understood that he was trying to make up for our troubled past, even though he never came out and said it. Watching him interact so patiently and lovingly with the baby, I began to see the kind of man and father he was capable of being.

But the carefree times ended abruptly one balmy day that August. After an afternoon of shopping, my father and I arrived back at the apartment building laughing over a new nickname. The doorman came up to us in the lobby. It was clear from his expression that something was very wrong.

"I had to drive your wife and daughter to the hospital," he told us soberly. "The baby is very sick. They're at Westminster." He went on to tell us that Michelle had come down with a high fever and convulsions.

That was the beginning of a heartrending month-long vigil. My stepmother slept in my sister's hospital room each night on an uncomfortable cot. My father and I visited every day. Each afternoon he and I would trudge back to the flat, discouraged and lonely. Michelle didn't seem to be improving, and no one could pinpoint exactly what was wrong. We were no longer our playful selves. I knew Dad, like myself, felt guilty that we'd been out shopping and having fun when the baby got sick. His stony silences made me understand even more how much he cherished his new family, as he lived day after day under the threat of losing it. And I was just as scared. I adored my baby half-sister, and missed playing and laughing with her.

Fortunately, my sister made a full recovery, although to this day we don't know what made her so sick. Eventually she was able to leave the hospital and then return home with us to the United States. She is now a healthy young woman in her twenties, just as I was that fateful summer.

Our father passed away ten years ago, a heavy blow to each of us. That time in London seems a lifetime away, but I will forever remember its full range of emotions; the joy and lightness as well as the worry and fear. Looking back, I realize it was actually in the difficult times that my father and I grew closer, not in the times when we were having fun.

I know something else now, too. The summer of nicknames was the summer I finally met my dad.

CAROL E. AYER (who will no longer answer to "Pigs") lives in Hayward, California. She has been published in *Woman's World* magazine, *The Prairie Times*, two *Chicken Soup for the Soul* books, and on numerous websites.

Use Your Brains

ELISE TEITELBAUM

D ad,

  The suspension-bridge-
  Cat-walking-
  Civil engineer,
  Home for a rainy April weekend,
  And I, the five-year-old daughter, spread out IBM keypunch
cards on the frayed but vacuumed living room carpet. This, our
first game of Battleship, marked a lifelong quest to educate me in
the family tradition, unmindful of childhood authorities.
  "What's one plus one in base two?" Dad said. "Quick."
  "Ten."
  "You got five toys. I take away six."
  "Can't."
  "Can. It's negative one. Means I owe one."

The guests we practiced for, my father's friends, rang the doorbell—*Bing-bong!*—early. Dad watched in dismay as I ran to the door. He disdained gifts, especially toys, except for the plywood airplanes, orange-crate chessmen, go-carts, and kites built at home.

Gifts and more gifts, wet and shining, piled up like wind drag loads on the Manhattan Bridge, which Dad said would soon collapse. Because the fourth law of thermodynamics called Murphy's Law says that what can go wrong, will go wrong, the loads fell down.

One box fell into the hands of my father's friend's daughter, too young to know it wasn't hers. Dropping packages and candied fruits, I whacked the box and threw the girl down.

"It's hers! Give it!" Dad, mistaken of course, shouted at me.

"I had five."

"Take away six!" Dad said, gathering each gift, worthless in his eyes, for confiscation. "You have negative one!"

"Can't."

"Go up and don't come down!" My father said—defying Newton's law of gravity and the way of the world. At that moment, for all intents and purposes, the party ended.

Even in the 1930s, Dad broke rules. Smart people had license to do so. My young father rode the backs of municipal trucks and trolley cars like bucking broncos. On a dare, he jumped across a six-foot-wide excavation hole and lived. He hailed from the land of cliffs, snakes, and lions—I mean home of the zoo, the Bronx. This meant Dad, like King Solomon, held a key to the homes and languages of orangutans from Indonesia and alligators from the Everglades. When an animal got hungry, Dad bought peanuts. When I got hungry, we drove up the Grand Concourse to Grandpop's apartment with a loaf of rye bread and a bottle of schnapps.

Grandpop survived on a pension from the painters' union, which had once assigned him to paint the Waldorf Astoria Hotel. From that time on, his apartment emanated grandeur. After offering Grandpop his tribute of schnapps, Dad showed me the carved mahogany claw feet he'd polished every week as a boy. He praised the health and dignity of Grandpop's subsistence on rye bread with onion, a diet Dad approximated when Mom left me in his care.

By fourth grade, I refused any more of my father's help. Interest in animals, nature walks, plywood airplanes, and kites smelled, in school, of delinquency.

"Here," Dad said, stirring a spoon of Ovaltine into a pot of milk. "Let's fix the problem. Five plus seven. First, let's do that in base five."

"Not now, Dad—please."

"I send you to school and you forget math?"

"Miss Leo said to stop changing bases."

"Tell her to shut up."

"I can't."

"She can't stop your brains."

"Daddy, stop!"

The phone rang. It was Grandpop, mugged in the Bronx on the way to deposit his pension check. Dad ran for his coat.

After resettling his father in a place across from our house, Dad remembered my birthday. I wanted a folk guitar. He bought a mahogany cutaway steel twelve-string instrument, too shiny, red, and embarrassing for public use. Unaffected by groans of protest from Mom and me, Dad threw in some albums, Andrés Segovia's Bach and Charlie Parker's bebop songs.

Dad turned on the classical music station. "Who composed this?" he demanded.

"Who cares?"

"It's Brahms." Dad bought the record in case I'd forget.

Dad marked me the lone survivor of a tribe that placed family above friends, science above entertainment. No one could deter him—except a man I'll call Wizard, the school psychologist who agreed with the social worker, who thought Dad crazy for yelling at Miss Leo for disallowing his daughter to think. So, under the weight of bureaucratic pressure, Dad, Mom, and I visited Wizard for tests, meetings, and therapy.

As Wizard's fortunes rose, Dad's fell. Wizard moved to a suite on 72nd Street. To go there, I needed a bus and three subways. In Wizard's view, one plus three added always to four. To be mentally healthy, I had to stop thinking about math and think about boys. What fantasies did I have? None?

"Tell me your dreams."

"I dreamed about cats."

"Cats represent boys."

The more I listened to Wizard, the more I thought about boys, and the angrier Dad felt toward Wizard. The angrier Dad felt toward Wizard, the more Thorazine Wizard prescribed for

Dad. When the Thorazine didn't work, Wizard prescribed shock treatments. When shock treatments didn't work, Wizard said Mom should lock Dad out of the house, and somehow or other Mom first changed the locks and later changed her mind and let Dad in.

At last Wizard said I should transfer to a boarding school, with boys of course. As for Dad, I broke off phone contact, letters, and visits.

Something over the years, I didn't know what, went wrong. Though I followed other girls' ways, married, and moved far from home, the farther I moved the smaller, more boring the world became. The one to fix it could only be Dad, the man of spirit who frowned on materialism, transcended personal desire, and jumped over barricades. I heard his voice: Fire the servants. Quit the tea parties. Use your brains. Do it yourself. I followed Dad uphill and jumped in the shadow of dangerous cliffs—divorce, poverty, remarriage, mountains and mountains of trouble. But when the Wizard called for the children, I surpassed my father's ferocity. ❧

ELISE TEITELBAUM moved from upstate New York to the Negev Desert in time for society to collapse in the Year 2000. Still waiting for that to happen, meanwhile Mrs. Teitelbaum produced two plays and a story that won first prize in the 2004 Moondance Film Festival. She lives with her engineer husband, a child prodigy, and, among others, a kid who plays basketball.

For the Things He Taught Me

GARY LUERDING

Dad would laugh uproariously if he thought I believed him my hero. Still, he would be flattered. Not only was Dad my hero, my confidant, and my best friend, he was my teacher, and he taught by example.

When I was old enough he taught me how to shoot a rifle and later to hunt. "If you wound an animal you need to find it and put it out of its misery no matter how much time it takes or how far you must hike." Dad proved that to me on our last hunt together. As a deer hunter, he was woefully unlucky and I believe he didn't really want to kill a deer. But one year he managed to bring down a medium-size buck. He was jubilant until he came up to the animal. It lay there unmoving, its large eyes looking fearfully up at my dad. After he dispatched it, he knelt down and wept. It was the last time he hunted deer.

My dad taught me it's okay for a real man to shed tears. I saw his only twice. That last deer hunt and when my parents divorced.

He loved my mother until the day he died, and I was grateful they still remained close friends for the rest of their lives.

And he taught me tolerance. The first time I came home from school with skinned knuckles and a bloody nose, Dad asked me what happened. "Darrell pushed me in the lunch line and I hit him," I said.

Dad became angry. Darrell was my best friend. "Do you think that solved anything?"

"I dunno," I replied.

"Gary, sometimes just walking away is the best course of action, especially among friends. Is one moment of satisfaction worth the loss of a friendship?" I later apologized to my friend, and we remain close to this day.

He taught me never to hit a woman under any circumstances. "Gary, those who do are the lowest of lowlifes. All of them, no matter how big, how strong, or how intimidating, are cowards down to the last man."

Of course, at the time, I didn't think these things were heroic and maybe they weren't. I was just a kid and later a teenager not wise enough to understand even though I thought I knew it all.

And he taught me patience. I enlisted in the army and when I came home on leave Dad bought a Labrador Retriever pup and named her Sandy. He never trained a hunting dog in his life; nevertheless, that's exactly what he set out to do. He'd write letters telling of his progress and I could tell Sandy had become more than just a mere hunting dog. To him, she was his companion and friend. He told me of his now solitary duck hunting trips spending cold nights in his pickup camper with Sandy curled up by his side while a pot of pork and beans heated on the stove. He'd share them with her, and wrote, "Oh my Gawd, I had to sleep with the door open! I love her to death, but you gotta draw the line somewhere!"

Several years later, again on leave, I got to see Sandy work the fields. She was a marvel to watch. He seldom spoke for she responded to his hand signals. He'd gesture left—she'd go left, etc. When she came upon game, she'd stand stiff, her tail straight out, her nose inches from the ground. "Get 'em girl," he'd say, and she would charge into the brush, then stop short as she flushed the birds.

Wherever he went, Sandy was by his side.

Due to my army career and my overseas embassy assignments, our separations turned into years. Each time I returned I found him getting older, but he never slowed down.

When he retired he bought a small house in a peaceful valley in southern Oregon. This land is rugged and filled with an abundance of fir, pine, and cedar trees. After a lifetime of city life, it was just what he wanted.

We stayed with him for a couple of weeks in 1973 while on leave. Dad, my wife, our three small children, and I would often sit on the porch at night and look at the clear starry sky while listening to the rustling of the trees. Dad called it his "river in the trees," and if you closed your eyes you could imagine yourself sitting beside its banks.

He encouraged us to buy acreage next to his and his face would light up describing the happy times we would share. "Have you taught the boy to hunt?" he said, gesturing toward my son, John.

"Well, no, Dad. He's only five," I replied. Then he reminded me I was just a bit older when I accompanied him hunting for the first time.

By now his beloved dog, Sandy, was very old. Her muzzle had turned white and, like Dad, she walked kind of bowlegged. He even had to help her up the three steps to the front porch. One day as Dad, Sandy, and I sat in front of the house, Sandy got up on shaky legs, her muzzle sniffing the air. She could barely walk but she went into a trembling "point" nevertheless. Soon a bevy of mountain quail came out of the brush. For Dad (and me), it was heartbreaking. "Her body is frail but she's all heart . . . kinda like your ol' man," he remarked, lightly punching me on the shoulder.

"How many years have you got left in the army?"

"Three more, Dad," I said.

"Well, don't waste your money building a home. Add on here. That is if you don't mind living with a crotchety old man." As a military family, owning a home, even a shared one, was a dream we never thought possible.

Those three years passed swiftly and when we returned Dad seemed to have aged more than the years we'd been gone. "Damned old age is catching up to me," he chuckled. "Better than the alternative though, right?" I agreed and he laughed and handed me a cold beer.

We spent the down payment we saved for our house on his. And all through the dust, dirt, and noise of remodeling, and with the kids running in and out slamming doors, he never once complained.

One night, as we sat on the porch, he said, "I don't regret my life. I do regret I won't have more time with you and my grandchildren. However, I'm glad of one thing, that you and your family will always have a home. I've made the last payment on this place and now it's yours."

Two weeks later he was gone. ❧

GARY LUERDING is a retired army NCO. His writing has appeared in five *Chicken Soup for the Soul* series books, *A Cup of Comfort®*, and numerous newspapers. He is also the author of *Inshore Ocean Fishing for Dummies*.

Priceless Treasures

KATHERINE HEDLAND HANSEN

Every time you ask my dad what he wants for a gift, whether it's for Father's Day, his birthday, or Christmas, the answer is inevitably the same: "Just make me something."

He loved the footstool I hammered together and varnished in elementary summer camp, and the brown and orange snail my sister made by sticking a bunch of nails into a piece of Styrofoam.

My dad wasn't pretending—he *really* loved those things, and wouldn't part with his treasures for anything. During a recent visit home, Dad proudly brought out the lacquered footstool and offered it to my one-year-old son. He keeps the guitar-playing girl I molded from green clay in elementary school in the china cabinet. Somewhere in the house are macramé plant hangers, a hooked rug lion, and a leopard-print ceramic cookie jar—all works of art created by his kids.

To us, they serve as reminders of the dad we adored, the one who gave my sister, brother, and me rides in a wheelbarrow when he could've just finished the yard work, and the dad who donned ridiculous pink and grey bunny ears and hopped around the neighborhood hiding Easter eggs.

When he built a sandbox for his kids, our dad didn't settle for filling a square of two-by-fours with some dirt. Instead, he created an elaborate red building, complete with a roof and windows. We spent many happy hours in our special clubhouse, holding secret meetings and making mud pies. Our dad even sacrificed a large, round section of his perfect green lawn to construct a homemade ice rink.

He also made up bedtime stories and sang to us at night, strumming the guitar he taught himself to play. I didn't know then that the lyrics would be ingrained in my memory or that the lessons would be passed down through generations. But I still sing those same songs on road trips today, and the "Abba Dabba" tune I loved as a little girl elicited some of my son's first real giggles.

For every occasion, our dad gave us books with brief but poignant inscriptions, and all three of his kids became and remain prolific readers. When I was in fourth grade, he told me if I read the newspaper and watched the news, he would vote for the presidential candidate I recommended. From him, I learned the power of knowledge and the importance of voicing my opinions, which had a lot to do with why I became a journalist.

Dad also taught me about benevolence. One Thanksgiving, Dad drove us to the store to buy turkey and all the fixings. Then we went to our church to leave the groceries for a family who had none, and proceeded to spend our Thanksgiving enjoying hot dogs with our cousins.

All throughout high school, a woman with spiky platinum blonde hair and black lipstick cut my hair. I didn't know at first that she had been a client of my dad's who needed help but didn't have money for a lawyer. He had accepted payment in free haircuts for his wife and kids.

Once my sister found a diamond ring in a parking lot, and Dad helped her place a lost-and-found ad in the paper. When the grateful owner offered a monetary reward, Dad instructed my sister not to take it. "You don't get rewarded for doing the right thing," he told her.

These values have stayed with me throughout my life and continue to shape my actions and interactions, but we may have learned our most important lessons about love and loyalty from my dad's relationship with my mom.

My parents shared a deep and powerful love that carried them through almost forty years of marriage. When they spoke their vows, I'm sure they didn't predict what life would bring them: the good (successful careers, three children), the bad (particular moments with same three children), and the worst (disability and disease). My mom still had a toddler when she learned she had multiple sclerosis, a cruel and unpredictable disease that steadily robbed her of her mobility, and her fierce independence, over the next thirty years.

Between her fighting spirit and my dad's constant and unselfish support, Mom continued to do as much as she could. When she was diagnosed with pancreatic cancer—an unbelievable blow to us all after all she had sustained already—Dad preached hope. "We're going to fight this," he reassured her. But it proved too much and when we lost her, even while enduring his own indescribable grief, Dad worried more about his children—now grown, but still not ready for a motherless world—than he did himself.

Even her doctors and nurses had commented on their abiding love. "We've been talking about you," my mom's oncologist had informed my dad. "And what we've been saying is, 'I hope my husband loves me as much as you love her.'"

I wish everyone could grow up with a father who loved his children as much as my dad loves us. When I went to the hospital on Christmas Day and was told I needed to deliver my baby right away, my dad hopped on a plane and arrived at the hospital in the middle of the night, just in time for the C-section birth.

After the first night, my dad sent everyone else home. I was a little concerned that I might need help with some things that my husband or sister might be more comfortable doing, but I need not have worried. Dad repeatedly got up and shushed the baby, brought him to me to nurse, helped me in and out of bed, and continually checked with the nurses on my condition.

That night, as my dad and I sat together in the wee hours, exhausted but marveling at the miracle in my arms, I told my father he was a remarkable man. Then I whispered to my son how lucky he was to have a grandfather who would teach him silly songs and big words and life lessons—and who would never want more in return than a picture made from Popsicle sticks.

KATHERINE HEDLAND HANSEN is a former reporter and editor who currently works in communications.

Fireworks

JUDITH FREELAND

"**B**ut Daddy," I whined, "we never go to the lake until after fireworks night." I had just learned that our family's summer vacation at a Canadian lake cottage would begin early this year. My brother's response to the schedule change was to stomp outside, slamming the door behind him.

My parents enjoyed the town's Fourth of July extravaganza as much as any kid, but the annual respite for them to swim, sunbathe, golf, and relax with friends was more important than any shower of rockets. Right then, nothing was more important to my brother and me than fireworks.

In a rare moment of togetherness, he and I came up with a plan. This time it was my brother's turn to do the pleading. "Could we come back just for the fireworks?" he begged.

Dad gave the matter a few seconds' thought. We could tell when he'd reached a decision: His face set like granite. It would have been right at home on Mt. Rushmore. "No," he said. "We can't do an 800-mile round trip for anything but an emergency, and fireworks are not an emergency."

To pacify us, however, Dad said we could have our own private celebration. He even promised to buy some sparklers to take on the trip. We scorned the idea of just sparklers. We wanted the glory of blazing colors, brilliant explosions, deafening noises.

Dad reminded us that Canadians don't celebrate our Independence Day. My brother thought about that for a minute before coming up with a counterargument. "But, Dad, our lake friends would come to watch our rockets bursting over the lake. Everyone loves fireworks. Please, Dad?"

The granite face cracked, almost imperceptibly, but it cracked. He promised to think it over; I secretly thought he wanted to see rockets bursting over the lake as much as we did.

We bought sacks full of marvels from the glorious array of bomblets, rockets, firecrackers, sparklers, and fire fountains at the once-a-year stand that was set up near the airport, just outside the city limits. My brother and I fussed half of that afternoon, afraid that our supply would prove insufficient, that our celebration would fizzle. Dad took us both by the shoulders and made us look into his eyes. "Kids, I promise you the most spectacular fireworks you will ever see." Then I knew it would be okay. My dad always kept his promises.

Finally the big night came. To all the kids waiting on our porch, impatiently asking, "Isn't it ever going to get dark?" and all the equally eager adults who hid their anticipation somewhat better, the gradual darkening of the sky seemed to take forever. The afternoon's fitful breeze, that hadn't quite raised whitecaps on the ruffled lake, had died down, leaving the lake a sheet of dark glass. Another sunset, the kind that local and visiting artists tried fruitlessly to capture on canvas, had slowly faded away.

Then the dusk became dark, and off we trooped, down the gnarly tree-root steps of the hill to the smooth, still sun-warmed sands of the beach. Dad scampered down the hill as adroitly as the kids. All the families from nearby cottages gathered on the beach, circling my father and the treasure trove of fireworks. He barely noticed, intent on his job of fire master.

After he equipped each child and all willing adults with sparklers, Dad lit his own and then touched the one nearest him. Slowly an ever-widening ring of twinkling candles sputtered and fizzed in the quiet. From across the lake a loon called to its mate.

Then it was time for the big bangs. Dad carefully anchored the first rocket, aiming it high over the waiting water, and lit it. Nothing. A soft swoosh. A faint light trail up into the sky, and then the explosion that made everyone jump before the chorus of "Ooohs" as the rocket went nova in a widening circle of crimson confetti.

Each successive rocket and blaster and banger seemed bigger and better than the one before until, at last, Dad launched the final four show stoppers simultaneously, and red, yellow, blue, and purple spheres merged and were reflected in the mirror of the lake, and it was over.

The neighbors called their thank-yous and good nights as they disappeared into the trees on the way to their own cottages. Our family stayed to tidy up the beach, stuffing burnt-out sparklers and the fragments of rocket blasters into trash bags. We were almost finished when Dad stood up, gazing across the lake.

Looking like all the veils of Salome, pastel ghosts were shape-shifting all across the northern sky—pale yellow merging into soft, faint green, replaced by a tissue the color of the midday sky, sliding into a haze of purple, then shadow-crimson. From east to west, horizon to zenith, the ripple of colors danced. In the deafening silence, I reached for Dad's hand, breathless.

The aurora borealis had quietly, proudly, breathtakingly filled the sky over the lake with Mother Nature's awesome answer to our puny human light show.

Gradually the colors faded until only murky white veils shimmered across the expanse of sky. And then it was dark. Still holding my father's hand, I remembered to breathe, returned to Earth.

Dad had promised the most spectacular fireworks ever, and he always kept his promises.

JUDITH FREELAND, as a mother, grandmother, and great-grandmother, has been careful to promise children only what she can deliver. As a college professor and administrator, she was careful to promise only grades that were earned and promotions that were merited. Now retired, she keeps promising herself to take life easy—sometime.

Be Quiet . . . We're at War

RONALD HURST

Joseph Brookes, my granddad, gladly served as my father figure. Rough-skinned, worn, and calloused, his hands could do anything. Those also gentle, loving hands often comforted me in my childish troubles. They even helped my father build a beautiful writing desk out of old tea chests. In daily use for many years, that desk became my only link with my father, who died from tuberculosis in a miserable slum in Sheffield when I was two years old.

My granddad's hands also comforted my mother through those dark days, and again when we gathered around the radio to hear the prime minister announce that Britain was at war with Nazi Germany. Later that day, Granddad passed us as we played noisily in the street. "Be quiet. We're at war," he said, raising a finger to his lips.

It seemed a silly remark to my six-year-old ears. How could Hitler hear us? Germany was miles away.

Having experienced the horrors of the First World War, Granddad was already mourning the deaths to come.

Born in 1882, Granddad trained as a bricklayer, like his father and grandfather before him. A fine craftsman, he dreamed of building elegant homes and stately buildings. His employers wanted those hands to build more slums.

After the First World War, things changed for the better. Granddad helped build homes fit for the returning heroes. The city council created vast housing estates around the boundaries of Sheffield and began to demolish the slums. Those were good times, but they did not last for long. The Great Depression came in 1929, and Granddad was out of work. In desperation, he took a job maintaining the furnaces of a large steelworks.

Light spongy firebricks insulated the steel outer casings of the furnaces from the intense heat inside them. The firebricks wore out quickly, and the bricklayers replaced them. To save money, the men were ordered to work inside the furnaces while they were still hot. If they refused, hundreds of men eager to take their jobs waited outside the factories.

The interior of a typical furnace might be twenty-feet long and eight-feet wide with an arched roof no more than three-feet high at its center. The workers wrapped rags around their knees and hands to protect them from the heat as they knelt on the brick floor to bring down the arched roof with picks. They had to sweep out the dust from the crumbling bricks with brushes whose bristles shriveled in the heat.

My granddad's gentle hands became scarred and broken, but when the time came to replace the lining, he prepared and placed the bricks with the loving care of a craftsman.

By 1938, the hard and dangerous work had ruined Granddad's health. He weighed just 100 pounds and coughed incessantly. His right forearm had a huge ulcer, and for the last years of his life his arm was strapped to an aluminum plate for support.

Nevertheless, a panel of doctors refused his compensation claim. They decided his illness had nothing to do with his work. He never worked again.

The blitz in World War II was an anxious time for Granddad. He had no access to telephones, and, for security reasons, the authorities gave only vague and misleading information about air raids. Granddad heard the antiaircraft guns and sometimes bombing during the night, but had no idea where the bombing was taking place. For information, he had to rely on Lord Haw-Haw, a collaborator who broadcast propaganda from Germany, or rumors. The only way Granddad could be sure we were all right was to come over to visit us. At that time, he lived with Grandma about three miles away from us. As the buses seldom ran after the raids, he had to walk six miles round trip day after day.

On one particular morning, he walked over amid the lingering stench of explosives, the smoke, and the gritty taste of pulverized brick that always followed raids. As he drew near to our house, he had to divert around areas the wardens had roped off because of unexploded bombs. He could not approach our house directly. I can only imagine his anxiety when the wardens told him that three unexploded bombs had landed near our home and trapped us in our shelter. He managed to work his way round to a point where he could get within fifty yards of us. At that point, soldiers ordered him back, but he pushed past them. To his right, a high iron fence blocked his way; he had to pass within a few feet of one of the bombs. He did not hesitate. Once he reached our air-raid shelter, he calmly led us past the bomb to safety. His one remaining good hand held mine in reassurance. We were able to use a circuitous route to his house and stayed there until the military removed the bombs.

A few weeks later Grandma and Granddad were the victims of another raid. A landmine exploded near their home killing dozens of people, destroying many houses, and damaging theirs. They were severely shocked but otherwise uninjured. That day, Uncle Joe, mother's only sibling, made the trip over to let us know they had survived. That was the only time in six years of war that Granddad did not manage to make the journey himself.

Granddad left me with few memories of direct conversations. However, I do remember overhearing a conversation he had with my mother. He described, with a deadpan face, how he had bought fish and chips wrapped in newspaper on his way over to visit us. The wind almost blew them away. He sat on a wall, holding them down with the elbow of his crippled right arm while he scooped the fish and chips up with his left hand. He made it sound as if it was great fun.

The ulcer on his arm was a red hole big enough to hold an egg. I once had the temerity to ask him what caused it. With that same deadpan face, he told me the doctor had blown it up like a bicycle tire, and it burst. Those were the only times I remember him mentioning his physical problems.

Though always in pain, he never complained. Shortly after the end of the war, he quietly died. Those amazing hands were stilled at last.

His union fought for many years to obtain compensation for the workers from his former employers. Even the union's brilliant young lawyer, Hartley Shawcross, made little headway—until the autopsy after Granddad's death showed clearly that his lungs were burned and clogged by silica dust from the furnaces.

Granddad never saw any compensation, but the precedent set by his successful case meant hundreds of workers who had suffered in the same way were able to get the compensation they deserved. It was typical of Granddad that even in death he served others. ৯৯

RONALD HURST credits his granddad with providing a secure foundation for himself and his two brothers. One of Joseph's grandsons worked as a steelworks foreman, one owned an engineering business, and Ronald went on to become a teacher and school principal. His granddad's skills and values were passed on to his numerous great-great grandchildren.

A Whap on the Head

C. LYNN BECK

"Did you hear that noise?" Mom said in a startled voice, sitting bolt upright in bed. The springs creaked slightly as she turned toward Dad and nudged him with her elbow.

"Uumph." His eyes remained closed and he breathed heavily, still half-asleep, unaware of the sounds that had seeped into her subconscious and caused alarm.

As she listened, the front screen door closed with a small click that reverberated through the quiet house. Their home had been broken into twice before, but never when they were inside. Mom leaned over Dad and shook him. "Wake up!" she whispered in a restrained hiss, her face blanching white with fear.

Dad's brown eyes popped open. "What's wrong?" His dark eyebrows furrowed together as he tried to figure out why she'd woken him from such a sound sleep.

"Someone's trying to get into the house!" Mom said, her eyes widening in the sparse light of the darkened room. "I heard them rattle the front door."

He sat up in bed, fully awake now, and tilted his head to the right, listening for sounds from the living room. Nothing.

Thump! This time the noise came from outside the bedroom window.

"What was that?" Mom whispered, fear tightening her throat.

Dad nodded his shaved head in the direction of the sound and put a finger to his lips. They both listened, faces turned toward the dark night.

The air was humid, and hot enough to cook black-eyed peas on the vine. During the seventies, most of the homes in the Washington, D.C., suburbs didn't have any air conditioning, so the window was open.

As they peered into the darkness, a small breeze stirred the curtain. Silhouettes from the streetlight threw shadow-puppet shapes on the ceiling. The thrumming of crickets echoed through the air while the papery buzz of cicadas created a background for the cricket concerto.

They continued listening while their hearts raced. Their adrenaline surged and their breathing became shallow.

Clunk. The screen popped off—pried from the outside and deposited on the ground below.

Dad moved the bedcovers back, the sheets crumpling noiselessly to the side. Sliding out of bed, he crouched down and picked up a short section of two by four from the floor. Normally, when the windows were closed, the board served as extra security—jammed in the window's track. Holding the board tightly, Dad blended into the darkness of the room, his olive skin acting as camouflage.

The intruder's shoes scraped against the wood siding as he climbed his way up the wall. Labored breathing marked his progress as he hauled himself higher and higher.

Soon, his fingers curled over the edge of the sill. The top of his head moved into view—

Dad reared back with the board and slammed it down on the man's skull—whap!

With a yell, the intruder dropped to the ground. He stumbled and swayed for a few minutes, holding an aching head that was rapidly developing a large goose egg. Bent with pain, he staggered off into the night, swearing a blue streak and waking the dogs in the neighborhood.

Mom's instincts leaned toward flight, but Dad's were always finely tuned toward fight. As a teenager in the city of San Francisco, he'd learned street smarts. Twenty years of military service and a tour of duty fighting in Vietnam, toughened him even more—but it never turned him into a braggart.

When he came home from Southeast Asia with medals, I asked him what they were for, and he said, "Saving someone's life."

"Whose?"

"My own. I jumped under the bed when the shooting started," he said with a teasing note in his voice. Then he laughed and changed the subject.

That same tough guy—who could scare my boyfriends off the porch with just one look—actually hated killing anything. I once found an injured rabbit and begged Dad to help it. With sadness in his eyes, he told me its back was broken. Then, despite his dislike for what needed to be done, he offered to put the rabbit out of its misery so that I wouldn't have to do it.

When the incident with the intruder happened, a 9mm Luger sat next to the bed and a .22 pistol lay in his dresser drawer. Sometime later, I asked him why he hadn't picked up his gun and used it. He said, "I didn't need to do that. The guy was probably just some drunk—who didn't realize he was at the wrong house—and when he couldn't get the front door open, decided to try the window."

In his typical way, he treated the incident casually—as nothing more than an attempt by a drunk to sneak into the house without his irate wife catching him. That's the way my dad handles life—cool under pressure and brave in the face of fear—and that makes him more of a hero than any medals ever could.

C. LYNN BECK is a freelance author/humor columnist with stories published in newspapers, magazines, and books. She lives in Utah with her husband, Russ, and their dog, Corky Porky Pie, who freely offer unsolicited opinions on her latest work in progress—a coauthored book of humorous anecdotes. For information about her writing, visit her website at *www.bythebecks.com.*

Save the Children

TIM ELHAJJ

On one of our first car trips of the summer, I switch to radio at Dad's request, and then start humming along to an old Simon and Garfunkel tune from the sixties. My window is open. I am watching the scenery go past with the wind on my face, when suddenly Dad turns down the radio. I cut my eyes at him, annoyed. As I turn the radio back up, Dad slaps my hand away and clicks it off.

"No man is a rock, son." Dad says this and points his index finger to the roof. "No man is an island."

When Dad tries to sound profound, it makes me feel self-conscious. To make myself feel better, I consider telling him he has the lyrics wrong. At the last second, I decide to just smile and nod my head. "Cool," I say.

Dad wants to talk about my behavior, but I don't have any explanations for him. I hum songs about feeling lonely and isolated, as if they were theme songs written expressly for me. Any irony in the lyrics about what happens to people who feel this lonely and disconnected sails right over my head. If he is going to reach me, this is what my father must overcome.

"You think," Dad says, "you're not as good as Tom and Tony, but that's not true. You're just different. You can do things those two can't."

Looking out the window, I pretend what Dad is saying doesn't even matter to me, but I am listening carefully to every word he says. The wind rushing in the window makes a loud noise. I wait quietly for a few minutes. When I finally speak, my voice sounds creaky and dry.

"Like what things?" I ask.

I have waited so long to speak that my father is caught off-guard. As he stumbles for words, I click the radio back on, keeping the volume low.

"I don't know," Dad says. "Drawing? Reading?"

Bad answer. My interest in these things is well known, but both have proved to be poor substitutes for athletic prowess. I look at Dad with such disdain he immediately begins searching for something else to say. After a few minutes of hedging, Dad zeroes in on one thing with confidence.

"You can make small talk," Dad says.

I look at him warily. I am not even sure what small talk is, but at least it is unexpected. I sit quietly while Dad recounts an incident that happened weeks ago when his sister called, but his hands were full, and he couldn't take the phone. I chatted with her about the weather and school for a few minutes. Small talk.

"That doesn't sound too important, if you know what I mean."
I tune the radio to a pop station I like.

"Your brothers can't do it! If they took that phone, they'd be like two lumps on a log."

I patronize Dad with a smile. I like hearing him call Tom and Tony lumps on a log, but this small talk thing sounds desperate. "Come on, Dad."

Putting my hand out the window, I let it coast in the rushing wind. Dad protests about the inherent value of small talk for a bit, but then he sighs. He gives up and the car goes quiet. On the radio an advertisement plays for a charitable foundation called Save the Children. It must be a well-funded campaign, because the radio stations play this ad constantly.

I am humming along with the radio when suddenly my father's hand comes crashing down on my thigh. I look over and he has a wide grin.

"You," he says, "*are* special."

His hand clutches my stinging thigh, and he squeezes hard enough to make me wince. "And you're going to do something none of the others can do. I know it."

I turn my head so he can't see me grin. When I have my face under control, I look back again.

"Like what?" I ask.

I know this question puts him on the spot. I know I probably shouldn't even ask, but I can't resist. Waiting patiently, I look to him for an answer.

He thinks for a minute and says, "Save the children."
I laugh, astonished.

"That's a radio commercial," I say. I am looking at him incredulously, but still chuckling. "You just repeated what was on the radio."

"Doesn't matter," Dad says. "It's important. And you're going to do it." He grins at me. There is nothing in his manner that suggests he is unsure, despite how stupid it all sounds.

I am pretty sure he is patronizing me but not completely certain. I don't know how I feel. Finally, I decide I am annoyed. I tell Dad to cut it out. To just quit.

"It's a commercial," I say. "Stop."

"You don't want to save the children," Dad says. "Alright. Don't." He keeps his eyes on the road. I hear the rhythmic thumping of the tires on the highway.

"Sit on your ass," he mumbles quietly to himself.

When I hear this, I feel exasperated. His disappointment consumes me. I find myself wanting to explain to him why I cannot save any children. Then I realize how ridiculous it is to justify this nonsense with an explanation, and I give up. The car goes quiet. I feel a mixture of relief and frustration. I tell myself I can at least feel grateful we have put this uncomfortable conversation behind us. There is the tiniest hint of disappointment, lingering at the back of my mind. No sooner do I think I have won, than Dad's big hand comes crashing down on my thigh again.

"You're special, son," he says. "I know it."

He says this with such enthusiasm and sincerity it takes my breath away. I have to use both hands to push his meaty palm off my thigh, but even two-handed, I never try too hard. I can't. I have to keep turning my head away, so he can't see me grinning.

For the rest of that summer, "save the children" becomes a sort of code between us. I never say it, but I long to hear it from him. When Dad says it, I always do one of two things: I either turn my head away and grin, or I search Dad's face to see if he is pulling my leg. Although I look often and hard, I never find any hint of insincerity there. ✺

TIM ELHAJJ studied fiction with Alice Sebold and nonfiction with Louise DeSalvo. Currently working on a coming-of-age memoir, Tim takes frequent breaks to write about his elementary school kids, parenting, and a past life shooting dope. Find out more about Tim from his website, Present Tense (past imperfect), at *www.telhajj.com.*

Whittling Words

CAROL L. MacKAY

As I sat there, listening to my father's eulogy, I knew the whole truth wasn't coming across. But I didn't speak up, didn't respond to the minister's request for stories. The whole time I held a story that, to me, exemplified my father. And I didn't share it. Instead, I listened as my father was recounted as a silent man who placed value on work over relationships. It's true. Words were not my father's forte. He was a "just do it" kind of guy.

My parents owned a variety store in a small town, and we lived upstairs in the "living quarters." Dad was also a farmer with a quarter section about three miles out of town. On occasion I would go with him to the farm. He'd do his work; I'd do some exploring, most often in the old abandoned farmhouse. On one of my visits to the farm, when I was eight years old, I encountered a mouse as I entered the farmhouse and quickly retreated. I wasn't about to venture farther knowing a rodent was on the loose.

I walked down the lane to a clearing in a wooded area where my family sometimes had wiener roasts. My father was busy cultivating the adjoining field. I sat down on a tree stump and watched my father in his tractor as it went round and round in circles. To quell my boredom, I picked up a tree branch, and played Xs & Os against myself. A few games of that, and I was so acutely aware of how bored I was that I literally scratched words like *boring*, and *snoring*, followed by a string of zees. When I heard the tractor engine turn off, I looked up and saw the tractor door swing open and my father jump down from the cab.

Something was wrong. I was sure he'd start tinkering with the cultivator or fiddling with the engine. If my father stopped in the middle of fieldwork, there was a problem. I hated problems, or at least being around when there were problems. Sometimes problems that started out having nothing to do with you became your problems. So, when I saw my father, with his big work boots, puffing through the freshly turned soil toward me, I reviewed my last few actions. Stick. Dirt. A simple game of Xs & Os. I hadn't left the door wide open on the farmhouse. I hadn't touched any equipment. I hadn't said anything rude. The worst I could think of was the "boring" comment I made to myself, but he'd have to be a mind reader!

So I sat on my stump, wondering, but fairly sure I hadn't done anything. My father kept on coming, all the way from across the field and then right past me into the grove of trees behind me. I couldn't resist. I had to turn around to see what he was doing. He pulled out a pocketknife, sliced off a willow branch, slowly walked back in my direction, shaving off the shoots of the branch, and sat down on the stump beside me. I was completely baffled. A switch? Was he making a switch? I'd never seen a switch, but I'd heard about willow switches in stories. But then he started to whistle. One thing I knew about my father, if it was time for a licking there was no whistling. So what was he doing? I watched as he shortened up the stick, coaxed the bark off in one perfect cylinder. I watched as his leathery hands whittled impressions in the center wood, and made holes in the bark. His large fingers fumbled a bit as he tried to slip the bark back onto the piece of wood, but after a few tries he was successful and then tested his creation. He raised the whistle to his lips and blew. And then he handed it to me with a simple, "There you go." As I watched him walk back to the tractor, the whistle cradled in my palm, I knew then, even as an eight-year-old, what it was he had actually had given me.

Sitting there, listening to my father's eulogy, it occurred to me that I have inherited some of my father's traits, as he had, undoubtedly, inherited a few from his parents. I, too, have difficulty verbalizing my thoughts. But as I considered Dad's method of getting his message across, I realized I have my own way of expressing myself, too. Dad whittled me a song. He did what he could do, and showed me how I could do it, too. Now it's my turn to whittle a few words out of willow bark and press them onto paper. I can only hope that someone will hear the song in my words. ✺

CAROL L. MacKAY is a children's writer and poet from rural Alberta, Canada. Her poems and stories have appeared in literary magazines across North America and Ireland.

The Shadow

JULIE McGUIRE

Five-year old Sebastian and his seven-year old brother Alex scrambled out of the car at day care. "I think you look like the Shadow, Daddy," Sebastian said.

"Maybe I am," my new husband Matt said in a low voice, his bushy eyebrows raised. He winked at his adopted sons, hugged them close, and told them he loved them.

"Love you too, Shadow," Alex said, giggling.

They wrapped their arms around me with an abandon that never failed to surprise and delight me, and then scurried to day care. Walking back to the car, I studied the man who, two years before, had responded enthusiastically to my online personal ad, and soon confidently embraced our ready-made family. My sons' biological father had long ago disappeared from their lives— Sebastian had never met him—and so the boys soon easily called Matt "Daddy."

On the morning Sebastian dubbed him "The Shadow," Matt was wearing his usual winter costume: a long black wool coat, with a bright red scarf wrapped around his neck and mouth to keep out the bitter cold. Perched on his bald head was a black center-dent fedora. His hazel eyes, ruddy cheeks, and long nose lent him an aristocratic air—perfect for a 1950s-era superhero.

Matt had passed his childhood passion—comic books and superheroes—on to the boys. The three of them often surfed the Web, gathering information about their favorite superheroes. They soon amassed a large collection of comic books and action figures. Our bookshelves were lined with old issues of DC and Marvel comics. We had even decorated the boys' room with images of Spiderman, Wolverine, Thor, Captain America, and their favorite—The Shadow.

Alex, a fact enthusiast, once pointed out, "The Shadow doesn't really have super powers. But when he puts on his fedora, he becomes invisible and clouds the minds of bad guys."

Sebastian, more interested in style than substance, said, "I think he looks cool."

As Matt drove me to the subway on his way to school, I noticed a grin on his face. "Honey, what are you thinking about?" I asked.

He looked confused for a moment; he'd been lost in his own world. "Oh, I'm thinking about talking about superheroes in class today," he answered, grinning.

"Are you going to ask the students about their favorites, that kind of thing?" I asked.

"Actually, I was thinking about how heroes have changed since the 1950s. I'm curious how high school students define heroes, whether they even believe in heroes, super or otherwise. I'm curious which historical figures they consider heroic. Superheroes are usually portrayed as ordinary people given extraordinary gifts. They provided inspiration for nerds, like me, who weren't strong like the jocks. Think Clark Kent and Peter Parker, perfectly ordinary, nerdy human beings. Even Wonder Woman was powerless without her magic lasso. . . . "

"When I was a child, our neighbor had a prized 1929 Ford Model A," I said, interrupting. "One morning the jack slipped, and the car fell on top of him. His eighty-two-year old wife heard his screams and raced out of the house. And she lifted the car off him. She saved his life."

"Exactly," Matt said, nodding. "Profound love, intense fear, strange and unusual situations can cause human beings to rise above their weaknesses, to do the unimaginable. If anyone tried to hurt you or the boys, I think I'd be capable of just about anything."

The sincerity in his voice brought tears to my eyes. "It's a great topic for your students, honey."

At the subway, I wiped chocolate from the corner of his mouth, and checked his coat for donut crumbs, and then kissed my superhero goodbye. He's off to make the world a better place, I mused. To say it had been love at first sight would sound cliché, except it was true. Sebastian, Alex, and I fell hopelessly in love with Matt, and he with us. He's not perfect. He's messy. He's a picky eater. He's absent-minded and clumsy. Some would say, eccentric.

No, not perfect, just perfect for us. When nightmares disrupt their sleep, Matt becomes their own personal superhero, fighting off monsters and ghosts, and chasing away the Boogey Man. When bullies make fun of Sebastian's bright red hair, or tease Alex about being small, Matt reminds his sons that character is more important than physical characteristics. When terrorists attacked the World Trade Center on 9/11, Matt reassured our sons that he would keep them safe.

"Protecting my family is my job," he'd said.

But Matt isn't just a protector. He's a father figure, who teaches our sons about integrity and honesty. Through his actions, he guides them to be compassionate, thoughtful young men of good character, and consistently proves that fatherhood is more than blood deep. Matt may not be the Shadow, but the boys believe he has super powers. Decked out in his coat, scarf, and fedora, I have to wonder sometimes. Did the Shadow have someone to wipe chocolate from his mouth and check for donut crumbs on his coat?

JULIE McGUIRE is a litigation paralegal by day and writer at heart. Her published essays and poems have appeared in publications such as *The Christian Science Monitor*, *The Birmingham Literary Journal*, and other small periodicals. She is a book reviewer and fiction editor for the *Internet Review of Books*, and a freelance writer for *Work Magazine*. She lives with a superhero and their two sons in Richmond, Virginia.

Foxhole Fathering

ANNA AQUINO

When my nineteen-year-old father was shipped to Vietnam, in 1967, during the height of the war, a grunt soldier's life expectancy was extremely short. Within fourteen days of being dispatched to the jungle, far too many American sons returned home in a pine box. My dad, Kenneth Palmer Jr., survived his entire tour of nine months in the bush, dodging bullets, swimming through rice paddies, being exposed to leprosy, and learning to laugh in the face of insanity and disaster. Though he'd been drafted and thrown into the pits of hell, the horror of war failed to break him.

I didn't learn until I was an adult that my dad had even been captured and tortured for several days. His POW days came to an end when my ingenious father escaped by working his way free from the bamboo pole they thought could hold him. Then, à la James Bond, he skulked into the void of a dark and lonely jungle—my father is a survivor.

When we were little, my sister and I would sit at our father's knee and listen to the same war stories over and over again. He loved to tell us stories, but only the funny ones like when he had to run up a tree because he tried to feed a baby water buffalo his C-rations and its mother didn't like that one bit. Daddy had a way of bringing those stories to life so vividly we could almost see the charging water buffalo, and in our hearts, we ran too. When he told us of the rice paddies serving as the public toilets, the smells of our bean, potato, and sausage dinner took on an air of old urine. When he told of his friend who cherished a tin of popcorn sent from home so much he refused to throw away the tin, he showed us how that tin echoed in the jungle, and we heard the echoes too. Through him, we experienced the rhythm of the jungle mixed with the sound of a drum.

When our father told us of having only a few months left in his tour and being offered a desk job, we sighed when he told us he turned it down because he couldn't walk away from his men in the field. We were innocent and didn't understand his sense of duty and honor; to us, they were little more than dictionary words that might as well have been written in invisible ink.

Sometimes Dad would be in the middle of a story and stop abruptly, as if he was again watching a friend lying wounded or dying in front of him. He would pause and regain his composure; he never told us the bad parts, but we could hear sadness in his voice. I never left the security of his lap, but I grew up in the red fields of Vietnam too. His tenacity is etched deep in my soul.

My dad will say that he's not a hero. He'd say that people who call themselves heroes are inflated glory-seekers whose combat experience consisted of moving a pen and a pencil around on a metal desk. He'll say the heroes are the ones who didn't come home. He'll say the heroes are the ones that suddenly died of lead poisoning brought on by an unexpected bullet. But my dad *is* a hero. He chose to survive, and every day since, he has chosen to live the gift of life that was so many times almost taken from him.

He gamely displays his medals neatly on a bedroom wall. He earned: three Bronze Stars, a Silver Star (that he never received), and a Medal of Good Conduct. But if you ask him about them, he'll say the only one he really earned was the Medal of Good Conduct. He'll laugh and tell you that one of his commanding officers nominated him for it as a joke. But when I stand in front of all those medals I see his courage; I see his strength; I see a man whose eyes have seen too much; I see a man who surrendered his freedom and sacrificed his innocence so that others might be free.

These days I love to tell my children about their grandfather's heroism. I tell them the same stories, and they laugh in the same places where my sister and I used to laugh. I tell them because I don't want my girls to ever forget my father's heroism. Sometimes, at night I sing verses from "Where Have All the Flowers Gone" to lull them to sleep, just like my dad did for me. And sometimes I cry for all the soldiers who didn't survive, who sacrificed their lives. In the same breath, I give thanks for my father and all the many heroes whose blood, sweat, and tears made this nation great. Many were boys who came home men and fathered very lucky children.

ANNA AQUINO lives in Central Florida with her husband, two children, and one fish. She is the author of seven books, four screenplays, two children's book series, and one women's devotional. Her father's story of survival in Vietnam inspired her first book.

The Day Will Rogers Died

KATHRYN THOMPSON PRESLEY

I t was scorching hot that August day in 1935. Spindly cotton
plants wilted in the fields and my sun-suit clung to me like
moonflower vines clung to the porch. We ate our usual meal of
red beans, fried potatoes, green onions, and sliced tomatoes. Papa
had washed and picked the beans the night before by lamplight,
and put them on to cook after breakfast on the back of our old
wood stove. I helped him clear away lunch things and set the
table for our supper which would be clabber milk with cornbread, cooked after the sweltering heat subsided so he wouldn't
mind firing up the stove.

After dinner, we rested on the front porch a while, listening
to cicadas buzzing in the trees and hawks "kerwheeing" overhead.
Our little two-roomed "shotgun cabin" sat high on a bluff above
the Washita; if there was any breeze at all, it always came up across
the river and cooled us on the porch. But there was no breeze
that day, so Papa hoisted me to his shoulders and headed for the

cotton patch. Since my mother was still in the charity hospital up at Oklahoma City, Daddy took me with him everywhere. Only later would I realize what a strain the care of a young child must have been on a struggling cotton farmer.

We had a lot riding on the cotton crop that year; a mortgage payment was due in November. But it had not been a good year: blazing sun, very little rain, and great, dark dusters blew in from the northwest. Papa stooped down to examine a cotton stalk just as the 2:00 P.M. train came meandering up the Washita valley. Most days, the engineer and brakeman were our only contacts with the outside world. We waved and yelled at them like they were long-lost kin, and they waved back, sometimes delighting me by tooting the train whistle. Now, they yelled something incomprehensible and pitched us a special edition of the *Daily Oklahoman*. When Papa saw the bold, black headlines, he knew what the trainmen had tried to tell us. Wiley Post and Will Rogers had gone down in a fiery plane crash near Point Barrow, Alaska. Some nameless Eskimo had run three hours to reach civilization and spread the tragic news.

Will Rogers was our hero, our friend in an unfriendly world. Though he had become famous as a rodeo star, actor, and home-spun philosopher, he remained a simple Oklahoma cowboy at heart. One of my father's proudest moments came when a neighbor told him he looked a lot like Will Rogers. Years later, I found dozens of Rogers's aphorisms copied laboriously in my father's handwriting on the back of an old wall calendar:

"When the Okies left Oklahoma and moved to California, they raised the average intelligence levels in both states."

"Everybody is ignorant. Only on different subjects."

"My ancestors didn't come over on the Mayflower; they met the boat."

In 1935, I couldn't understand why Papa looked so stricken and wouldn't understand for twenty years or more. But I knew something was terribly wrong. Wordlessly, my father gathered me up again to ride on his shoulders as we headed toward home. Silently, he set me down on the dusty porch and went in to the kitchen table. He sat there for a long time, his arms folded on the table. Then, he put his head down on his arms and wept. I had never seen my father cry.

I understand now that he wept for Will Rogers who was Cherokee like himself, and who had the courage and wit to speak the things poor folks wanted to say to politicians in Washington. While Will Rogers lived, we had a voice in the world. No Oklahoma farmer could be a total failure as long as Will Rogers spoke for us. Old Will never met a man he didn't like, and we loved him for that.

Papa also wept that day for my mother, shattered in body and mind, and he wept for me. I had never had a doll except those made from cucumbers or corncobs, and on that summer day, my future looked bleak. He wept for the farmers who had watched their crops burn up and blow away, for everyone who couldn't pay their mortgage.

He didn't make cornbread that night, didn't light the fire at all; we ate a bowl of cold beans and sat on the porch listening to whippoorwills down by the barn. Ordinarily, we would have gone for a dip in the river or bathed in the washtub behind the smoke house. But that night, for the first time in memory, we went to bed without bathing. We slept on our pallets on the porch, and I roused up twice during the night, once to the sound of coyotes yapping down by the river. The second time, I thought someone was sobbing, but that could have been a bad dream.

My mother came home two weeks after Will Rogers died. She had spent most of my life in hospitals, and I was not particularly glad to have her back. She was nervous and irritable and had trouble holding food down. I'd grown accustomed to having Papa all to myself and Mama complicated our lives. I heard my aunts whispering words like "morphine" and "crazy." They didn't know back then about postpartum depression. I only knew she cried a lot and didn't seem to like me much. She stayed in bed most of the time, and pretty soon, I was going to the cotton patch with Papa, just as I had always done.

It took only a few days to pick our sparse cotton crop that year, and after paying a little on the mortgage, there was $55 left in the bank. Grimly, my father did the chores, tended our livestock, and did the cooking and housework. Over the weeks and months, my mother slowly, very slowly, returned to health.

The Great Depression hung on a while longer and dust storms known locally as "black blizzards" still blew in occasionally from the west, but that terrible day in August 1935 seemed a kind of turning point for our family—a nadir from which the only direction was upward. With little education, no money, no resources except his faith, integrity, and a loving heart, my father labored to hold our family together. His pastor's eulogy described him well: "Blessed is that man who loves his family and his work, with whom all are comfortable, and in whom his children see God." ❧

KATHRYN THOMPSON PRESLEY is a retired English professor living in Bryan, Texas. She has published poetry and dozens of stories in national magazines, professional journals, and anthologies. She teaches Bible studies and has been a conference speaker for decades.

Ruffling Feathers

WAYNE SCHEER

You should have had a raucous wake, the kind you see in movies. A bottle of whiskey should have been passed from mourner to mourner, as each told stories about you, embroidering the details with each swig. We should have all gotten drunk, even the women and children. Songs should have been sung, and fate should have been cursed. A fight should have broken out between your grieving brothers. One should have wrestled the other to the ground while family screamed and friends cheered. Then, amid the blood, broken chairs, and torn suits, hands should have been shaken, men should have embraced, and tears should have flowed as freely as the whiskey.

But none of this happened, of course—because you were a Jew and Jews grieved silently, privately, worrying what the *goyim* would think, acting more like guests tiptoeing around the house trying not to make too much noise than mourners cursing fate. Thus, your funeral was quiet, somber, and uneventful.

But Dad, in your quiet way, throughout your life, you made some noise, you ruffled your share of feathers. Although I never saw you cry, nor raise your voice in anger, you aroused more emotion in others than you ever knew.

Until the day she died, Mom missed you so much she cried herself to sleep every night. And Lisa suffered through a bad marriage because her husband couldn't measure up to you. Maybe now she's found a good one. We can only hope.

And me, the rebellious son, the one who left home as soon as he could, renouncing your religion and your parochial ways, I think of you more than I care to admit. How can I help it? I see your face in my mirror every day. As my unruly hair turns white, I see your tight snowy curls. I keep mine longer than you ever dared, letting my hair hang below my collar, still defying your unassuming, above-the-ears cut.

I see your eyes in mine, covered by trifocals like the ones you wore and hated. I see the same small, piercing brown eyes that dart around, taking everything in while offering little expression. I sensed intelligence behind your eyes, wisdom, but you were always reluctant to share what you were thinking, perhaps afraid your ideas were too bold.

I remember as a child fishing from a small rowboat with you and your friend Mike. As the sun rose, you pulled a tiny black prayer book from your tackle box and asked Mike and me to hold the boat steady while you stood up, knees wobbly, and recited the prayer for the dead in Hebrew. It was the anniversary of your father's death and on that day at sunrise and sunset you stopped whatever you were doing to say the prayers.

Mike pointed at you and whispered, "You see the respect your father gives his father. That's what a man does." But later, while Mike was busy reeling in a flounder, you also whispered to me, "I said those prayers for my father because he would have wanted me to, but it's a silly tradition, and I don't want you to do that for me. I don't want you to remember the day I died."

I was ten at the time, but I never forgot that moment because you revealed something of yourself to me that we never spoke of again. And although—to honor your wishes—I've made a conscious effort not to remember the anniversary of your death, I think of you often. I miss you, particularly now that your grandson has children of his own.

You and I had our differences—what father and son hasn't? You pushed me to do well in school, sometimes pushing harder than I liked . . . and I pushed back. We had our words, although our arguments were always understated and careful, neither of us willing to cross that imaginary line. We fought over sports and politics. How you could have supported the war in Vietnam I'll never know. But with all of our fighting, I always knew you loved me, although once I was an adult you never expressed it in those actual words. Showing emotion didn't come easy to you. I understand that now, as I struggle to express my love to my adult son.

I remember saying "I love you" once. The cancer had reduced you to a mere skeleton, and you were in the hospital. We stared at one another, uncertain what to say or how to say it. When the nurse finally administered the dose of morphine and your face relaxed as the drug, momentarily, freed you from pain, I said, "I love you, Dad." I hope you heard me.

They say that time helps us heal and forget the past, but it's not true. As my son's dark, curly hair begins to show specks of white, and as I play with my grandchildren, I miss you more than ever. I wish now I could take back the harsh words we shared and return, just for a moment, to when I'd curl up on your lap and kiss your stubbly end-of-the-day cheek.

Standing at the cemetery, looking out at the neatly arranged tombstones, I recall how you discouraged me from saying kaddish, the prayer for the dead. Even if I could remember the words, they wouldn't suffice. I long to shout and scream and curse and get drunk and punch someone in the face. But as much as those emotions churn inside me, I won't rant against death. You see, Dad, although I've ruffled some feathers myself, I, too, am a quiet man.

WAYNE SCHEER taught writing and literature in college for twenty-five years, and then he retired to follow his own advice and write. He's been nominated for a Pushcart Prize and a Best of the Net. His work has appeared in *The Christian Science Monitor*, *Notre Dame Magazine*, *The Pedestal*, and *Eclectica*. Wayne lives in Atlanta with his wife.

Beethoven, Jersey Tomatoes, and Whales

SUSAN J. SIERSMA

With every deed you are sowing a seed, though the harvest you may not see.—Ella Wheeler Wilcox

On steamy July afternoons, tired from hours spent weeding rows of tomatoes and squash in my father's vegetable garden, I begged, "Daddy pleeeese, lets go swimming." I wanted to be like other kids whose parents took them to the beach or community pool. After complaining that it was far too hot to go anywhere, Dad packed my little brother, Joseph, and me into his rickety car. Then off to the river we'd head. It was on those sweltering afternoons, paddling our arms in the swift currents, that Joseph and I learned to be strong swimmers.

Why can't I have a normal father? I often thought to myself. While our friends visited parks and zoos, my siblings and I frequented the backyard with Dad acting as guide. Butterflies, ants, spiders, and assorted critters became lessons of the day. Our father fed crows and squirrels, songbirds, and chipmunks, even an occasional passing pheasant, all the while instilling a strong respect for animals in me and my brothers and sisters.

Although our childhood house was dilapidated, Joseph and I delighted in rolling marbles down its warped floors. Let's just say that Dad wasn't someone who could be called exactly *handy.* Uncovered septic pipes and mole mounds crisscrossed our front lawn. Summer nights carried hordes of flying bugs through holey screens into the upstairs bedrooms; winter found the windowpanes frosted from poor insulation. The back steps heaved, the front porch sagged, but my house always felt like home.

"How big is a whale Daddy?" repeatedly I asked my father. "Oh, a whale is as big as a football field" was his standard answer. Because the property across the street was similar in size to a football field, I continually imagined a giant whale lying across it.

"I want to travel like other kids do with their families," I'd say.

"Susie, a good book will take you *anywhere* in the world you want to go," Dad replied; he virtually devoured books. Actually we were fortunate to have our very own "library" in the front hall of our home—a crooked dresser that stood at the foot of the stairs, overflowing with used books. So many nights, I drifted off to sleep with a book in my hand, thinking, *why can't I have a normal father?*

On spring and fall weekends Joseph and I loved to depart on expeditions to the nearby fishing pond. Our poles amounted to nothing more than sticks with attached strings; night crawlers were the customary lure. After snagging several sunnies, we proudly carried home our loot. Friends snacked on corn chips or pretzels.

On the contrary, we feasted upon Dad's version of our catch of the day—bony sunfish dredged in flour and fried in butter. Surely angels above developed the recipe for that heavenly concoction!

In my past there were no piano or ballet lessons and movie outings were almost nonexistent. But as a young girl I danced to the classical music my father listened to on his radio. The melodies of Beethoven, Strauss, and Mantovanni filled the rooms in our aging home. Jean, my eldest sister, and I are still stirred whenever we hear the sweet notes of the Moonlight Sonata.

The word *normal* is defined as usual and ordinary. Nowadays when I ponder the question, "Why couldn't my father have been normal?" I know if Dad had been ordinary or usual, I might not have such a strong love of nature, an appreciation of toads and apple trees, of jack-in-the-pulpits, and swallowtails. Would I know the peace, the tranquility found in a day spent near water? And surely, if my father were "ordinary" my current garden wouldn't be so large. Some days, I'm convinced there's Jersey tomato juice flowing through my veins instead of blood. Most likely I wouldn't be the reader I am either. The shelves of my home are filled with myriads of magazines and books. Would I have learned one of life's best, most beautiful lessons—that music reaches where words cannot? And most importantly, how would I ever have known that a whale is as big as a football field? ❧

SUSAN J. SIERSMA, contributing author to several *Chicken Soup for the Soul* and *Cup of Comfort*® anthologies, enjoys time spent with her three children and five grandchildren. She also relishes long walks with her husband, Rodger, and pet therapy dog, Jack Sparrow.

Pop's Album

KENDA TURNER

Black-and-white photos "pop" by adding hand-colored accents. If, in a background of gray, a single tulip is highlighted in fuchsia or clouds are edged in violet and peach, facets of beauty, focus, or mood are emphasized. Color any element that begs attention and see what the picture tells you.

Special memories in the snapshots of our lives do the same thing. I learned this from my Pop.

I called my father "Pop" from an early age, trading the nickname for one he used for my sister and me. "Morning Glory," he'd say as we came downstairs for breakfast. Once he looked around the table at Mom, Sandy, and me and said, "Well, if it isn't Myrtle, Girdle, and Turtle." I don't remember who was who, but I do remember Pop's fun sense of humor.

Yet tough times tested Pop's gift, and as I embarked on the craft of hand-coloring photos, I reminisced about some of the challenges Pop had faced, especially in health and on the job.

One quiet day as I experimented with oil pastels and colored pencils on black-and-white prints, I also found myself imagining an album of my life with Pop. A color here and there "popped" as I recalled special memories. I savored them as I mentally turned page after page.

I first imagined a photo of a toddler snuggled on Pop's lap—me after falling down the stairs. Pop was the one who picked me up. It wasn't the only time he reached out to comfort. There were also long nights of rocking me as a feverish baby cutting teeth, or the time I fell and sorely bit my tongue, necessitating a trip to the doctor. "The tongue is the fastest part of the body to heal," the doctor said, and he sent us on our way. I'm told that Pop and I sat together in the big chair that same night and snacked on, of all things, salty potato chips. *Yellow* popped in that picture—for a child's golden hair, potato chips, and trust in a father's care.

Next was a blurred image of two young daughters waiting expectantly at a supper table covered in an orange-flowered tablecloth. Mom was sick that night and in bed upstairs. Sandy and I were hungry. All Pop could find to whip up for dinner was tomato soup made from puree, but it was enough. That page came to life in shades of *orange*—in homemade soup, flowered tablecloths, and reassurance that comes from a father's commitment.

A fun likeness followed. I could see myself as an elementary school student, sitting at a cafeteria table with my plaid lunchbox before me. Pop, who worked for the district at the time and had an office in my school building, often ate his lunch in the same room. One day he walked past and patted me on the shoulder. I smoothed my school-girl dress, opened my lunchbox and smiled, feeling quite special. *Red* popped up there—for little-girl dresses, plaid lunchboxes, and quiet confidence coming from a father's personal attention.

On still another page was a photo of the old house on Rose Hill. Originally a four-room cottage, the house had been expanded as the family grew to include two sons, and had its share of problems. Money was often tight. Yet the house, decorated outside with lavender irises, echoed inside with voices, euchre games, reunions—and Pop's ongoing joke every time the house needed paint. "This time," he'd say, "we'll paint the house *poi*ple." *Purple* packed a punch—for home, flowers planted alongside, and a father's devotion to family.

Album pages flipped image to image, recalling accumulated miles on the road with Pop behind the wheel. Not only did he freely pick me up from after-school activities, he was the one who took me to get glasses, or for orthodontic work. Along the route to the dentist we always passed a peacock farm. Proud birds strutted their stuff, displaying fans of jeweled feathers. The first time I saw them, I thought I was in an exotic place but Pop, who lived in real time, took care of the business of driving. That page sparkled in *turquoise* tones—for peacocks, steering wheels, and a father's willingness to be available.

Memories turned with the passing of years. Snapshots of happy times interspersed with sad. I saw myself all grown up and being escorted down the aisle by Pop at my wedding. Later he held his first grandchild, a little boy in blue, and four years later babysat his first granddaughter dressed in soft pink. Yet another image showed pale roses of the same color, fragrant and sadly sweet, on display at Sandy's funeral. She herself had suffered ill health for years from complications of diabetes. But Pop was there, in good times and bad, his support unwavering. *Pink* showed true in memories of babies, roses, and a father's loving dedication.

A final color "popped" in my imaginary album with the picture of Pop's first grandchild, our son now grown and engaged, when he traveled cross-country in the spring of the year to introduce his lovely fiancée to the family. Pop, recovering from yet another surgery, made the difficult trip to meet her. Images on that page resonated in *green*—for renewed springs, emerging life, and hope for the future.

In art, the color black adds contrast, perspective, value, and depth. In the same way, struggles and difficulties lend dimension to life. My family will continue to add snapshots to our album. Soon there will be pictures of Pop's first great-grandchild, a new face whose colors will start out in pastels and then graduate to all the bright hues of a color wheel.

But pictures among the pages of Pop's album will remain favorites. For there I've found love autographed in endurance and enhanced by such strong lines as humor, commitment, dedication, and hope. Just turn the pages of a life's album and see all the character-colors that pop!

KENDA TURNER lives and writes in Cincinnati, Ohio, and has been published in several periodicals. She enjoys photography, knitting, and scrapbooking—and reminiscing with Pop about the old days.

The Last Lesson

ALAN C. BAIRD

The mountains all around Tehachapi were booming.

It was early spring, and the sun warming the large rocks and empty hillside fields was so hot the air shimmered. Heat waves rose and merged into columns, some of which twisted into dust devils, mini-tornadoes of no particular threat except to scare the cows. But much of the rising air combined into large, swirling circles too diffuse to have the destructive energy of a tornado, but whose lifting energy was awesome.

The glider pilots call the large circles "thermals," just the ticket to a unique soaring experience. If a lightweight aircraft maneuvered into a thermal, it signaled the beginning of an elevator ride of perhaps several thousand feet, a vigorous acceleration that was much like getting a swift kick in the seat of the pants.

So, to a pilot familiar with the air conditions, the hills were booming with lift, a time when the glider pilots liked to say, "You can't fall out of the sky!" The current wisdom was that lift existed wherever you looked—just hire a tow plane to haul your gossamer wings to 1,000 feet or so, and you could ride all afternoon!

I had only recently re-entered the sport of soaring after a two-year layoff, and my skills were rusty. Even with the booming conditions, my flights would likely be short.

I had just graduated into a hot German fiberglass glider from the two-place, American Schweizer fabric-covered training glider, much as someone would take tentative hair-raising spins in a sleek, manual-shift Porsche after learning to drive in a beat-up old Ford automatic. I was torn—I longed for the high performance of the German aircraft but I also wanted the easy familiarity of a Schweizer.

My supervising instructor recommended a compromise: I had demonstrated adequate proficiency in the German glider—enough to give him the confidence to let me take out a single-place Schweizer. "The worst you can do is miss a thermal, embarrass yourself, and glide back down in twenty minutes! But I'd like to see you stay up for an hour or more, if you can," he said.

So I hooked the nose of the Schweizer 1-26 to a 200-foot tow-rope, and concentrated on staying behind the tow plane while it turned and climbed its way up to a particularly popular spot over one of the nearest peaks.

On the way up, I was so immersed in familiarizing myself with the 1-26 that I barely noticed the dozen gliders circling the mountain. Each tried to stay in a rising column of air that couldn't be seen; it could only be felt in the momentary rising of a wingtip, or, if they really had it pegged, that satisfying kick in the seat of their pants. Some of the pilots were doing very well; they flew in the same general area as several hawks. Since hawks are born to soar, by moving from one thermal to another with undetectable adjustments in their seemingly stationary outstretched wings, if those pilots could fly near the hawks, they were piloting admirably.

Finally, it was time to release from the tow plane, and to test my new acquaintanceship with the 1-26. Thunk! I watched the towrope recoil like a folding accordion, to gracefully trail behind the plane, now descending to the left. I made a climbing right turn to ensure that I would fly well away from the tow plane's path.

There! I sensed a slight nudge on the control stick as if somebody was trying to take control of the glider, and assumed a thermal was announcing itself, by pushing up on one of my wingtips. But, which one? It subsided within seconds so I pulled the glider into a tight, steep circle in search of that elusive nudge. And then—the kick in the seat of my pants! Whoopee! I gained 500 feet of altitude and longed to keep it up. If I could stay in this thermal, I would put several thousand feet of altitude in my bank, to squander later while searching for more lift.

Abruptly, it disappeared—a sinking feeling in my seat cushion, followed by a similar drop in the pit of my stomach. Instructors could teach patterns to fly in order to stay in the concentrated part of a thermal, but you almost had to have a sixth sense to keep your glider in a high-energy thermal for very long. I mentally kicked myself: "I can do better than this . . . my father taught me to do better than this."

That thought caught me by surprise. I hadn't thought much about my first instructor, my father, in months. And to be thinking about him now . . . when I was flying the same type glider that he so dearly loved to fly while he was alive . . . it was too much. My eyes filled with tears, and I turned the 1-26 back toward the airport. It wasn't such a bad flight; at least I kept it in the air longer than twenty minutes.

Then, suddenly, I caught a second thermal, and I distinctly heard my first instructor's voice from the back seat, "Turn left. Hard left." Automatically, my right hand swung the 1-26 into a steep left turn. You don't question your instructor's command—you just do it.

Sure enough, we had flown into the liveliest part of a dynamic thermal. Wahoo! According to the instruments, we rose 1,000 feet per minute. But it proved hard work to keep that one pegged; we slipped in and out of the strong lift. It required all my concentration to fly an unfamiliar aircraft in this wild, powerful thermal that was now a bucking bronco! I hoped the instructor in the back wasn't aware of my struggle. "C'mon, work it harder," again from the back seat. Damn. He noticed. I shut out everything except feeling the 1-26, and checking the sky for other gliders. The 1-26 and I merged into one entity—we fused at the control stick and had the flight of our lives.

I stole a glance at my watch and realized we had gained 5,000 feet in the last six minutes. The thermal was finally topping out and becoming easier to fly. I turned back over my shoulder to thank my instructor for the encouragement—and suddenly remembered that I was flying a single-place glider.

I felt dumbfounded. Someone had helped me. I had recognized that voice from somewhere. But it couldn't be . . . Dad had died two years ago.

Still shaken, I looked out toward the high right wing, still tilted up in a left turn to stay in the thermal, and saw a hawk eyeing me curiously and hanging in the sky, just a foot or so in front of my wingtip.

He honored me with his company for three full circles. 🐾

ALAN C. BAIRD enjoys referring to himself in the third person, and was inordinately pleased when ABC-TV's *Max Headroom* series purchased his debut student film, widely hailed as "the most noncommercial piece of **** in Michigan State's history." He is the coauthor of a hardback/softcover/web/WAP project entitled *www.9TimeZones.com*, which recently appeared at the Whitney Biennial. Born down east, Alan now lives just a stone's throw from Phoenix, which is fine and dandy, until the stones are thrown back.

A Quiet Carpenter

HARRIET PARKE

My father was a quiet man, a carpenter, a builder of houses, and a maker of furniture. I live surrounded by furniture he made for me: a tall grandfather clock in my living room that chimes every quarter hour (to the delight of my grandchildren), my bedroom suite of lovely Honduras mahogany (scarred over the years by my careless spilling of perfumes), the oak twin beds that my boys slept in, and a spinning wheel that actually spins.

My father built the basement of my childhood home, patiently, one cement block at a time. We lived in that basement as he built the rest of the house, slowly, buying building supplies when he could afford them. Aunts, uncles, and cousins would gather every weekend to help. The men held nails in their mouths as they worked, taking them out only to smoke Camels and Lucky Strikes. The women carried pitchers of iced tea to the men and served sandwiches on thick slices of homemade bread. At the end of the day, my father would build a bonfire and we would roast corn on the cob in their husks. The corn was from my father's garden, planted in long arrow-straight rows. I fondly remember the sweet-charred smell of that corn and the warm, wet feel of melted butter on my fingers.

After dinner, I would settle in to read the latest Trixie Belden novel, but would lay the book aside to watch and listen to the adults discuss, debate, and then loudly argue about who was a better president, FDR or Truman, the chances of the Pittsburgh Pirates to win the pennant, and the quality of Chevrolets versus Fords. The conversations grew more intense, more animated, swirling around the table like little tornadoes of sound. My father sat at the head of the table, quietly whittling a piece of wood, rubbing his thumb across the surface, smiling a crooked little grin that turned up only the left side of his mouth. He listened to the debates but stayed outside of them, on the fringe of the noise and the laughter. Even when my mother would demand his opinion, he would smile and shake his head.

I remember sawdust in his hair, on the backs of his hands, on the top of his shoes. I remember the smell of wood like an aura around him. Pine. Oak. Maple. But what I remember best and treasure the most about my father came later.

Born with congenital heart defects, my son suffered a head injury at age thirteen and a subsequent cardiac arrest. He was resuscitated but lay in critical condition in intensive care with an intracranial pressure monitor screwed into his head.

His prognosis was poor. Even if he survived, the doctors predicted brain damage. "Diffuse cerebral edema," the doctors said in mournful voices, shaking their heads. The nurses swabbed my son's shaved scalp, cleaning the skin around the intracranial pressure monitor screw, and then patted me gently on the back.

My father wouldn't come to the hospital. Quietly, but stubbornly, he refused, shaking his head, saying only that he would wait until later to see him. I didn't understand, wanted to scream, *There might not be a later.* I felt angry and hurt by his refusal.

Thankfully, over time, my son recovered. The barbaric pressure screw was removed from his head; his blonde hair began to grow back, stubble covering the scar. The respirator was slowly weaned away. He came home, thin and weak, but alive and alert. Very soon thereafter, my father came to visit—bearing a gift.

During those weeks while my mother, my husband, and I had hovered at my son's hospital bedside, my father—with sawdust in his hair and hope in his heart—had measured, cut, constructed, sanded, and varnished a magnificent golden oak desk and chair for his ill grandson.

Clad in his trademark bib overalls and flannel shirt, my quiet father carried the heavy desk into the house, up the steps, and into my son's room, and then, smiling, he went back for the chair. As we tearfully watched, my father knelt beside my son to steady and help him from the bed to the chair. My son's blue eyes—the same clear blue as my father's—glistened.

When I saw the same crooked grin exchanged between them, I understood why my father refused to go to the hospital. He had coped in the only way he knew how—by building something special for someone he loved. He had spent those dark days and nights in his workshop defying the prognosis, defying despair, defying grief by faithfully holding onto the belief that everything would turn out well, that my son would one day sit at the desk his grandfather built specifically for him.

HARRIET PARKE is a registered nurse who specialized in emergency nursing and emergency department management. She has been published in *Voices from the Attic* (a Carlow University anthology) and *Pittsburgh Magazine*. She also received an honorable mention from an *Atlantic Monthly* fiction contest.

My Defender

MARGARET LANG

*C*lank, *clank, clank.* Night after night, it kept me awake in the old, ivy-covered dormitory room. My friends said my pale, forlorn expression signified "sophomore slump." But I knew it was more than that. I had an armored antagonist in the form of a clanging radiator, determined to drive me either crazy or off campus.

He won't win this contest, I thought. Finally I could stand it no longer. Armed with a hammer, one night I struck what I hoped was a deathblow, and then twisted his calcified valves to the "off" position.

"There. That should keep you quiet," I said, snuggling under my down comforter on a subzero, New England night. Even with no lifeblood flowing in his veins, that cold, obstinate, wretched fellow still won the match. *Clank, clank, clank . . . clank, clank, clank . . . clank, clank, clank,* ad infinitum.

The janitor said, "I'm sorry, but the system is interconnected, so even if you took the knobs off, you can't really shut down your radiator."

My professor said, "Please don't sleep in class." Blurry eyes and fuzzy thinking were not helping my reputation, or my note-taking ability. And exams were coming.

My friends said, "We'd like to switch rooms with you, Margie, but. . . ."

The dean said, "Sorry, there are no empty rooms midterm."

"Actually a public park would do just fine," I mumbled, dragging myself across "College Hill" back to my cold room with its high ceiling and dark wood floor.

That night, as always . . . *clank, clank, clank*, my antagonist mocked me. The full moon, thankfully, had the good grace to bring Easter early that year, which meant a trip home. The thousand-mile journey only occurred twice during the school year, Christmas and Easter, and always by train. Boarding in Boston, I immediately converted the small slumber coach seat into a narrow fold-down bed. True to its name, sweet slumber was mine that night.

The next day, I disembarked at Chicago's LaSalle Street Station. Groggy, I collapsed silently into Mom and Dad's open arms. More typically, I would have heartily embraced them with a steady stream of chatter.

"What's wrong, honey?" asked Dad.

"Oh, nothing much," I downplayed my feelings so as not to alarm them. "I'm just a little tired; a noisy radiator keeps me up at night."

"A good night's sleep will do you wonders," Dad said, always the optimist.

I trudged up to the third floor of our brick colonial house. In the days when the home used to bustle with activity, my treetop room had been my favorite getaway place. Now my brother was married and away, our collie was gone, parties seldom given, and absolutely nothing stirred around the big house at night, except the wind in the elms. Still, secure sleep was all that mattered now.

Soon my body revived, but my spirits lagged behind. That annoyingly ironclad radiator loomed large; I could almost envision it viciously awaiting my return to college.

My doting dad tried to spark life back into me with gentle ribbing, a hug, a smile, and a positive word. His love arsenal had never failed to ignite my heart—until now. I didn't even sidle up to him, a gesture that would invariably cause him to drape his strong arm around my shoulders, pull me toward him and whisper, "Hello, Mugret." I had no sidling movement left in me.

Too soon, the dreaded day arrived. Mom waved the last goodbye to me at the station as I boarded the New England States train. Just moments before, my busy, corporate dad had been paged away on the loud speaker at the train station for a call from his office. I was sorry he couldn't see me off. Once seated in my slumber coach, I opened my books. *Before exams, this may be my last chance to study with a well-rested mind,* I thought.

The train traveled out of Illinois into Indiana. After a stop at Gary, it continued on its way. Well into the journey, I was dozing when I heard a familiar, dream-like voice. "Hello."

A tall, dark-haired, suited form of a man who resembled my dad stood next to my open compartment door. Stunned, I stared at him like I had seen a ghost. I glanced out the window at the scenery flying by, and then quickly back at him. *I left Dad in Chicago. How could he be here on this speeding train?*

His twinkling eyes and playful smile popped my eyes wide open. "Dad! What are you doing here?" I blurted out.

"Riding with you back to school."

"The whole way?"

"Yes, honey, the whole way. I even got myself a berth. Your spirits were down and I wanted to keep you company a little while longer. I waited for the train to be well out of Chicago so the surprise would be greater."

My handsome dad offered his arm and led me to the dining car, where an attentive waiter served us dinner on fine china, with silver place settings. I felt like a princess.

"Let's sit up in the club car long enough for me to smoke one cigar," Dad said after dinner. He knew how to draw out both conversation and a cigar. So happy in his company, I wished the cigar would last forever.

We reminisced about the time I was a child returning to Chicago from a visit to relatives that required traveling 600 miles by train alone. Dad had surprised me then by boarding another train outbound from Chicago to meet up with my train and ride back into Chicago with me—just so I wouldn't feel alone. What a joy it had been to lift up my sleepy head from the train seat, see his smiling face, and lean back against his strong shoulder. I was older now, but no less relieved.

Back at college I said goodbye to my one-of-a-kind father and watched his train disappear into the night. Later, snug in my dorm bed, my sleep was as deep as my heart was full. In my dreams, the *clank, clank, clank* of the radiator became the *click, click, click* of the train wheels. The intimidating radiator lost its final joust to my faithful defender—my dad. ✌

MARGARET LANG is an evangelist with Save the World Foundation in Africa, sharing the Gospel with thousands of school children each month. A published author of thirty-five stories, she loves to spin a tale especially about poignant moments in her life. Who better to write about, she says, than one she loved dearly—her father.

The Fall of the Nicotine Kid

R. GARY RAHAM

I have no idea what the Nicotine Kid's real name was. He regularly invaded "Roy's Coffee Shop" (Roy being my dad) to flirt with junior high school girls, maybe buy a burger and coke, and smoke—if he thought he could steal a puff or two in the parking lot. He wore a mostly white T-shirt, jeans, penny loafers, and combed his hair in waves that crashed together at the nape of his neck to form a rakish "ducktail"—the envy of all the pimply males a few years his junior. He also twisted a pack of Camels or Pall Malls into the right sleeve of his T-shirt. This both helped earn him his nickname and complete an iconic Beat Generation image. A somewhat overmuscled, probable high school dropout, he still radiated the coolness of the fifties like a living Marlboro commercial. Girls seemed to flutter at his approach like dinghies disturbed by wavelets of testosterone.

One girl got to know the edgier side of testosterone while dancing with him to the demonic beat of rock and roll emanating from the jukebox. The Nicotine Kid pushed her for some reason, breaking her necklace in the process. The mechanical arm of the record changer groped for another 45 as French fries froze midair. I remember the sound of beads clattering across the tile floor, and the faint fizzing of untended Coca Colas. My dad marched down the runway behind the lunch counter and latched onto the duck-tailed scruff of the delinquent's neck with one hand and a fistful of denim jeans with the other. He propelled the surprised adolescent out the front door and then literally rushed out to sit on him. Luckily, the Nicotine Kid wasn't built like a football hero, but then neither was my 5'6", 150-pound Dad.

I don't remember exactly what Dad said to him—only that it was a heated directive on how to behave around young ladies—but I remember feeling glad he wasn't saying it to me *and* so proud of him I puffed out my eleven-year-old chest.

Dad wasn't a violent man, which is why his actions surprised me. He was good for a swat in the seat of your pants if you misbehaved, but that was it. He assumed the role of stern father, I think, because that was what his nineteenth-century father had taught him—the eldest son in a family with five other kids. My Dad had not served in the military, being too young for the First World War and too old for the second, but he bore himself with that no-nonsense ramrod look that implied he was not to be trifled with. He kept his own counsel. He worked hard. And he dealt with my mother's asthma stoically.

Mom had acquired chronic asthma as a young adult. She lost three children after bearing my brother and sister. Her health dictated at least one medical abortion. She was doing well while carrying me, which meant I dropped into a family with two teenagers aghast at such a late and demanding arrival.

Mom took umpteen allergy tests, went to clinics, and used inhalants to control attacks, but that wasn't always enough. Sometimes, when she couldn't breathe at night Dad had to give her medication with an enema, often with me as an embarrassed assistant. I can see the heroism now that I couldn't see then in supporting the love of your life when she's battling for each and every breath and doing it with quiet assurance and without complaint.

My dad first met my mom when they were fellow employees in a Carborundum company in upstate New York. I treasure a letter he wrote back home to his folks from the Commodore Percy Hotel in Toledo dated March 7, 1928, the day they eloped. "I know you will be very much disappointed and I am sorry," he wrote, "but we are quite happy and I think it is all for the best."

And I think they were quite happy, overall. Mom liked to write poetry and on one occasion—probably my Dad's birthday sometime during the 1960s when I was attending college—she wrote a poem that concluded:

This big life puzzle is solved by a give and take deal,
A LOVE that withstands is one that is real.

Of course you can begin one jump in the lead,
Choose a life partner like mine—it's all you will need.

Dad had weathered the depression years as a salesman for an auto parts company, eventually earning a vice president's title. He became an American citizen shortly before the Second World War. When the boss absconded with most of the company's assets, Dad used what savings he had to buy the small candy shop/soda bar. Although only five at the time, I remember being mesmerized watching him make sundaes and flip burgers.

I can only think of one time I had to look at my father twice and briefly wondered if I had heard him correctly. Just before I left for college he chuckled nervously as he said what even I knew to be a cliché: "If you can't be good, be careful." Perhaps he thought he had to say something as I prepared to launch into territory unfamiliar to him. Perhaps his dad had said it to him, but for whatever reason I felt he had misjudged his impact on me.

Certainly I would be good. I would work hard, I wouldn't cheat on either my taxes or my wife, and I would do whatever needed to be done. Some actions—like sitting on the Nicotine Kid's chest and outlining right from wrong—are just non-negotiable when you've seen them ably and consistently demonstrated.

Perhaps the greatest gift my father gave me, though, was not a template for behavior. Bad or even flawed templates have to be unlearned or modified anyway. I'm most thankful that he didn't try to build me in his image or use me to probe paths he wished he had taken. Instead, he let me find my own strengths and grow into them, only delivering a swat in the pants when I wandered too close to the oncoming traffic of life. ❧

R. GARY RAHAM sees a few contemporary versions of the Nicotine Kid while visiting middle school classrooms trying to convince eighth graders that paleontologists and artists lead fun and exciting lives. He also writes an assortment of books, articles, and nature columns proposing that nature's book is a funny and worthwhile read. You can see his particular take on science, art, and nature at *www.biostration.com*.

Winged Victory

LINDA MARKLEY GORSKI

During World War II, ten brave young airmen trained together for six months to prepare for a combat mission in Austria. Because of their exceptional performance in training, their B-24 Liberator Bomber was selected to be christened *Winged Victory* to represent Moss Hart's play of that name about the Army Air Force. The cast of the play presented a special performance in New York City to honor the *Winged Victory* B-24 Liberator Bomber Crew.

The *Winged Victory* crew took off from New York on December 23, 1943. Their assignment: to complete five surprise combat raids over Austria. Following the success of their mission, the crew was to receive the Air Medal, return home to a ticker-tape parade, and tour the States with the *Winged Victory* play—an incredible honor for the crew and powerful propaganda for the United States.

Sergeant Joseph Edward Markley, the twenty-one-year-old Lead Radio Operator, was my dad. He graduated from high school in 1939 in Kitzmiller, Maryland, where he was the star center forward leading their soccer team to regional finals for the first time in their school's history. Kitzmiller offered two career options—working in the West Virginia coalmines or leaving town to find work elsewhere. On August 21, 1942, on a dare from two friends, Joe joined the Army Air Corps. Though it may have seemed daring to his friends, they were unaware that my dad often dreamed of flying in a silver bird.

On December 13, 1943, ten days before his journey overseas, his childhood sweetheart, Wilma Evans, traveled to Garden City, New York, where they wed in a small church.

When the *Winged Victory* B-24 Bomber Crew arrived in Cerignola, Italy, an eleventh man joined them. From their operating base in Cerignola, the crew successfully completed four missions in twenty-four days. February 25, 1944, the crew rose with the sun and took off in formation with three other planes for their fifth and final mission.

The crew never reached their primary target. After crossing the Alps into Austria, they became the target of German ground fire which crippled *Winged Victory* with direct hits on both inboard engines. Because the crew could not maintain the designated air speed or altitude, the other planes in the group formation gradually pulled away, reducing *Winged Victory* to easy prey for an ME-110 German fighter plane.

The pilot and copilot struggled to keep the crippled and burning bomber in the air, allowing the crew time to attempt an escape. The terrified crew began bailing out over Hollenstein, Austria. It was a bright, cloudless day, so they clearly saw their heavily armed captors below. The crew had no choice but to throw their arms high in the air and surrender. Six of them were captured immediately.

Later that evening they learned that one of their cherished comrades bailed out with a burning parachute, which collapsed. The bodies of the other four airmen, including the pilot and co-pilot, were found in the wreckage.

The six surviving *Winged Victory* crewmembers were held as prisoners of war for fourteen months and spent time in five different German prison camps.

Around 6:00 P.M. the evening of their capture, two German soldiers drove the six crewmembers to St. Polten Air Base in Austria. On the way, one of the survivors revealed that he still had his escape kit, with a compass, map, fishhooks and line, and forty-eight American dollars. He gave each survivor one of the bills from it. Once my dad got into a permanent camp, he sewed a five-dollar bill into the seam of his trousers. Though the others lost theirs in future searches, my dad had his when he was liberated, and we display it with a photograph of the *Winged Victory* crew.

In the early morning darkness of February 6, 1945, the German guards roused the weary, malnourished prisoners of Stalag Luft VI in Kiefheide, Germany, and started them off on the eighty-day trek that would come to be known as the Black March. The prisoners did not know that a truce was soon to be in effect—that this was a march to freedom—until April 26, 1945, when they came upon a small bridge that led into the town of Krina. The prisoners saw that on the other side of the bridge, the Germans were the prisoners and the Americans, the guards.

For my dad, the war did not end in Krina. For forty-three years, until the time of his death a few weeks short of his seventieth birthday, he was still waking in the middle of the night screaming for his lost comrades to "get the hell out" of the inferno.

From listening to his stories, reading his memoirs, and sifting through a treasure chest of documents he left behind, I learned important lessons about war from my dad.

Young soldiers mostly fight in wars. I can't imagine myself in my early twenties (or thirties or forties or fifties) having the raw guts that my dad did when he went off to war. On September 11, 2001, I was in the Pentagon when the terrorists crashed American Airlines Flight 77 into our building. Congress declared the Pentagon a war zone for that one day. I can't begin to express the sheer terror that we felt—and we weren't fighting; we were running.

Shortly after being captured, my dad and his five comrades were visited by a seventeen-year-old German flight gunner, the victor in their air battle. My dad said the young German shook their hands and said he was sorry, that he was just doing his job. My dad taught us that not all those wielding the weapons hate the individuals they are hired (or drafted) to fight.

Like so many young Americans during World War II, my dad went off to war a proud patriot. He came home fourteen months later physically and mentally aged. Yet my dad understood that what was at stake was our country. He stayed in the Air Force for over thirty years to ensure his comrades' sacrifices were not in vain. ✒

LINDA MARKLEY GORSKI was lucky enough to live all over the United States and graduate from high school in Okinawa in 1965, thanks to her dad being in the Air Force. She is a member of the Society of Children's Book Writers and Illustrators and the Charlotte Writers Club. Two seasonal quizzes she created were published in *BRIO Magazine*: The Christmas Quiz appeared in the December 2005 issue and How Much Do You Know About Easter appeared in the April 2006 issue.

The Grasshopper

HEIDI GROSCH

I've always had big ideas, sometimes seemingly impossible ideas. I can clearly see the outcome of something without knowing how to make it possible, although I am stubborn enough to think it will work somehow. Fortunately my dad, Ken Grosch, can plot out the details. He is as stubborn as I am, but has the patience to think things through and the determination to find a way to make it work.

"Dad, can you help me with my life science project? We have to make a three-dimensional model of something, including its insides!" I was thirteen and facing another daunting homework project. For once I hadn't left things until the last minute. There were still a couple of weeks before this project was due, but it was too overwhelming for me to face alone. Enter my hero, stage right.

My dad looked up from his latest fix-it project and smiled. "Of course I'll help," he said instantly, clapping his hands together. "Let's get to work."

"Now?" I questioned, surprised that he would drop everything to help me. I was also thinking about the Saturday morning's cartoon lineup, not sure I wanted to miss an episode of *Scooby-Doo*.

"No time like the present," he said, patting the stool next to him. We talked about all the possible things I could "dissect": an eyeball, the stamen of a flower, and the four stomachs of a cow. Finally I decided on a grasshopper. "Hold that thought," my dad said, jumping up from his stool and heading over to a corner of the garage. He returned with a piece of scrap siding. Sliding it across the workbench to me he declared, "Time to make a list!" I took the flat carpenter's pencil he handed me, flipping it over in my fingers. "Start by writing down everything you would find both inside and outside a grasshopper."

I scribbled down things like guts and skin, and then scratched them out when my dad reminded me this was a science project and needed to be accurate. A few forays into the house for the "G" *World Book Encyclopedia*, my textbook, and the dictionary narrowed down the specifics. (These were pre-Internet days so we didn't have the luxury of Google.) Hours later, surrounded by a small pile of scrap lumber now covered in lists, sketches, and measurements, we had a plan.

At this point many parents would direct their child to the craft cupboard for cardboard, construction paper, and glue. But not my dad. We headed to the basement, to his workshop, that magical place of bright lights and even brighter ideas. I had been there before, but that didn't make this excursion any less exciting. As I stepped inside that tiny room and heard the crunch of loose screws under my feet, I felt a little overwhelmed. Could this plan actually work? Could we really build a grasshopper? Then I looked over at my father, his shirt already covered in wood shavings, and I relaxed. He had made lots of things before with only a plan, and here he was, ready to help me make something too.

I drew out my grasshopper to scale on a piece of brown paper, and cut out its profile with a Saber Saw on a piece of masonite. The lines weren't quite straight but that didn't matter. My father was letting me do it; he was just there to make certain I didn't cut a finger off. "Ok, now we need a good foundation," he instructed. "Something good and solid so the grasshopper won't tip over." My dad has always been a big believer in having a solid foundation, whether in construction or in life.

We shaped an old metal window screen into the grasshopper's body and used plaster to cover it both inside and out. I painted our creation with an earthy brown and a Kelly green, old house paint I think, and we used colored pieces of electrical wire for the entrails. I was glad my dad never threw anything away; it really does come in handy some day.

My dad says we had a good time on that grasshopper project and that I stayed focused. I think he has to take credit for that. He made a boring school assignment challenging and fun. For many years that grasshopper was stored on the top shelf of the life science classroom in my old junior high. I was proud that the teacher thought it good enough to keep and even prouder of the dad who helped me finish it. We still enjoy working together on projects and can add to our list of joint accomplishments crafting flower pots out of old newspapers, repairing archaic plumbing once held together with black electrical tape, and installing a used stainless steel kitchen sink. His pile of scraps is still available for lists, and he always has a carpenter's pencil or two in his pocket, ready for the next idea. Thanks, Dad, for braving the schizophrenic mood swings of a teenager and for always being there for me, even in the seemingly impossible.

HEIDI GROSCH is grateful to her dad for teaching her to think creatively, a skill she has incorporated into her work as a children's writer and performer (*www.heidigrosch.com*). She is now using her creativity to drive on narrow mountain roads, learn Norwegian, and stack firewood in her new home on a Norwegian fjord. Her visits back to the United States are still filled with excursions to the basement, clothes covered in wood shavings, and projects with her father.

The Colonel to the Rescue

SUSAN REYNOLDS

Despite many nights spent wishing on a distant star, I never had a father protector, at least not until someone else's father unexpectedly stepped up to the plate. When he was present, my father was a large, imposing man who audibly scolded and physically punished his children—flaying bare bottoms with a leather belt strap—for minor infractions.

When I first met my husband, I was attracted to his prepossession, his confidence, and his bravado, but underneath his smooth façade, he contained my father's worst attributes magnified. He soon became an overbearing, verbally and emotionally abusive husband (and father) who created chaos and drama on a regular basis. I lived in fear of his booming voice, his angry red face, and his repetitive threats.

I hadn't known Paula very long, but from the moment we met, we had bonded over our love for our children (two each), our love for writing, and the disasters our marriages had become.

Once we began to whisper the truth into each other's ear, we both knew we had to abandon our marriages, and thus I first met Paula's father when she filed for divorce and he traveled from Indiana to California to protect her during a particularly tumultuous period.

Papa Colonel to his family and the Colonel to the rest of us, Paul Munier was a career soldier who had served in Vietnam. A cool, calm, collected leader among men, he was soft-spoken, subdued, and yet exuded an air of integrated confidence and hard-won manliness. One had little doubt that the Colonel was what he appeared to be—a strong, silent, wily, and fearless man. He was, in fact, the sane, silent counterpoint to my chest-thumping, domineering husband.

Things came to a brink one hot summer night when my husband and I returned from a marriage counseling session in which I had revealed that my husband used whatever I shared in our sessions as ammunition for four-hour fights in which he yelled and I cowered. Furious that I had exposed his real behavior, my husband picked up a twelve-inch solid, bulbous wooden statue and furiously and repeatedly banged it on the tile countertop. When I turned to look into my frightened children's faces, I knew I had to leave him—immediately.

I had already talked to a lawyer, so as soon as my husband departed on a business trip the next day, I called her and asked her to file papers I had presigned in anticipation that this day would come. When I reported the previous night's events, the lawyer insisted that we file the restraining order we had discussed and instructed me to withdraw half of our bank account.

After dropping my children off at school, I drove to the bank where I sat in the car for an hour, gripping the wheel, second-guessing what now felt like rash actions, and crying. Finally, in utter desperation, I drove to the nearest pay phone and called Paula's house. She wasn't home, and wasn't scheduled to return until the next day, but the Colonel, who had been around for months at this point and knew about my marital discord, immediately sized up the situation.

"Stay where you are," he commanded. Within minutes, the Colonel not only showed up, he drove me to a Mexican restaurant, listened while I whined and twisted napkins for an hour, bought me a lunch I couldn't eat and a margarita I downed quickly.

"Susan," he said, "Do you think there is any chance that your husband can change?"

"No," I answered openly weeping. "I don't."

"Are you prepared to accept the consequences of staying?"

I looked into the Colonel's eyes and knew that I couldn't lie to him, or to myself, but I also couldn't say the words.

"Your husband," he said softly, "is a formidable foe, and he'll never willingly surrender control. If this drama is going to end, it has to be you who makes the decision and sticks to it." I had, of course, had this same discussion many times with my therapist, and the marriage counselor once in a private session. My therapist had put it succinctly: "Your husband is controlling and abusive, and you deserve so much more . . . your children deserve so much more. He has squashed your dreams and your confidence, and he'll do the same to your children."

Remembering her words, I brushed unstoppable tears aside. "He threatens me constantly, and my lawyer is afraid he might harm me. If I do this, he'll go crazy, and I'll have to face him alone. I wanted my sister to come, but she called me today to say she couldn't come, and I'm afraid to do this alone."

The Colonel sat quietly, patiently, while I cried. He had been privy to conversations about my marriage, heard everything Paula had to say on the subject, yet I felt confident he had the most objective opinion, an opinion I could trust. Still, my heart thundered against my chest. "I feel like I'm not ready to make this final decision," I finally whispered.

"Susan," the Colonel answered soberly, "you made the decision weeks ago, and it's a simple truth that some battles have to be fought alone. I don't know you well, but I do know that you can do this, that you have to do this, and that it's time to do this."

"You're right, of course you're right," I answered, rising up, squaring my shoulders.

"Now," the Colonel said solemnly, without missing a beat, "we go to the bank."

Withdrawing the funds was a lengthy process, throughout which the Colonel stood by my side. When my hands shook, he put his hand on my elbow to steady me and silently waited until I regained my composure. When the clerks looked askance, as if about to question my right to withdraw the funds, he simply said, "This is also her bank account and her money," and then gave them a withering look that silenced them.

Without another word, the Colonel drove me home, stood guard while I stuffed clothes and toys into a suitcase, and then drove me back to my car. "Pick up your children and then come to Paula's," he said.

That night, when my husband returned, it didn't take long for him to figure out where I had gone. He came over to Paula's house and banged on the door demanding to see me. When the Colonel answered, he quickly changed his demeanor. "I would like to talk to my wife," he said politely.

"Ten minutes," the Colonel answered, and then followed my husband into the living room where he sat quietly, but pointedly, nearby. My husband dropped to his knees, sobbed uncontrollably, and begged me not to leave him, which both took me by surprise and weakened my resolve. When ten long minutes had passed, the Colonel stood up. "Time's up," he said tapping his watch.

I locked my eyes onto the Colonel's and knew what he was trying to tell me—that a few tears didn't indicate sincerity, only desperation. "I'm not changing my mind," I said, "and I would like you to leave."

Unfortunately, that was not the end of the battle; it was, in fact, merely the beginning. However, I never would have gotten that far that day without the Colonel, who saw a terrified young woman and stepped in to share his wisdom, his strength, his clarity, and his guiding hand. As I gave my husband a second, a third, and a fourth chance, twelve months passed before I finally filed the divorce papers. Throughout, I thought of the Colonel's actions and words many times, as I do today. He gave me the gift of backbone and the responsibility of knowing that when the battle lines are drawn and you know what you have to do, it's time to soldier up and take command of your situation. And if you're very lucky, you'll find a steely, softhearted Colonel standing right by your side, watching over you.

SUSAN REYNOLDS is a freelance editor and author. She authored *Change Your Shoes, Change Your Life*; *The Everything® Enneagram Book*; *The Everything® Guide to Personal Finance for Single Mothers*; *One-Income Household*, and *The Portable Italian Mamma*. She edited *Woodstock Revisited*, and is currently editing Adams Media's *Hero* Series. Learn more about Susan, and upcoming anthologies, on *www.literarycottage.com*.

Here's to You, Dad

DENNIS C. BENTLEY

I t was a rare event—three of the four adult siblings gathered around Mom's dinner table on Christmas Eve in rural western Kentucky. A couple of grandkids also there, strapped into battered highchairs stabbing at their finger food with sticky digits, their faces smudged and stained, their eyes glowing. The fireplace roared, the smell of burning hardwood blending with the savory aroma of all the right foods, perfectly prepared. Mom said grace, and we armed ourselves with her familiar mismatched utensils, taking aim and cautiously snagging the turkey and ham, ladling gravy onto everything.

Of course the phone rang. Of course it was for Dad. Of course someone had an emergency. Of course they were sorry to call so late on Christmas Eve—but they had no choice and knew of no one else to call. Without hesitation Dad cheerfully replied, "Okay, let me get some tools, and I'll be right there." And of course, he disappeared into the night—with a smile on his face.

The neighbors lived and celebrated much like we did—with the extended family gathered in a large ramshackle house with tall ceilings and ancient wiring and plumbing. Undoubtedly, their washing machine ran day and night, filled mostly with baby clothes and burp rags and burped-on shirts. Dad informed us—as he dashed for the door—that their machine had made an odd thumping noise just before water spewed from its backside onto the floor, at full flow, threatening to flood the kitchen. Of course it couldn't wait. Everyone knew Dad would have it under control in a matter of minutes. He had, after all, been fixing appliances—and just about everything else—since he was a kid.

After stopping the flow long enough to avert disaster, Dad rushed back to our house, rummaged through his stacks of cans and boxes in the basement, and then sped away again, with a used, but intact replacement hose. After installing it, Dad helped mop up the standing water, and then scooted the washing machine back into alignment. Of course, he chatted, joked, and laughed for a bit, and turned down money and food offerings before bidding them a happy holiday. That was Dad's way.

That no one in our family gave a second thought to Dad's willingness to put someone else's needs above his own—on a rare holiday when so much of his family was present—tells as much about my father as is possible in a single tale. That no one complained or said an ill word about it tells much about how we were brought up. It was quite simple: Someone needed help, and Dad could—and therefore would—take care of it. For Dad, there was simply no other option imaginable.

Born into abject poverty in the deep South, my dad's birth-mother had been forced to place him in a children's home. While still a young boy, Dad had been handed over to the charitable lady whose last name we bear. She was a widower with grown sons who had left home to raise their own families and tend to their own farms.

Like many of our fathers, mine recounted stories about walking several miles to a one-room schoolhouse—uphill both coming and going—through the year-round snow, driving rain, and parching desert-like heat. (My dad insists it is all completely true, and I wouldn't dream of calling this honorable and noble man an exaggerator.)

Dad toiled in neighboring farms to help support his aging adopted mother. School was hard and money was much needed, so Dad dropped out after eighth grade, never to return. Labor would become his career: farms, gas stations, tobacco auction floors, or whatever was available. A drought dried up his one attempt to run his own farm. Luckily, our mom remained at his side, good or bad, while also giving birth to four babies. Eventually a small business took hold, a niche was found: buying up old, obsolete gas-powered washing machines, fixing them and selling them (just above cost) to those who could not afford, or simply lacked the utilities to run, the newer electric models.

Soon came television sets—and another niche. The nearest broadcast station was forty miles away, the next, around sixty. A simple set of rabbit ears didn't have the reach to yank those signals from the sky. Towers, tall poles, and guy wires started going up in the late fifties, trending upwards through the early sixties.

Selling TVs and mounting antennas proved profitable; things for my family finally improved.

But Dad kept right on doing a multitude of odd jobs. Once, a freight elevator at a nearby store was acting up, so Dad naturally took on the repair job. When the cables tore, or slipped, and the flat, open car slammed to the basement floor, thirty feet down from where it started, Dad ended up with two busted legs and a broken back. The extended hospitalization massacred the family budget, and the business's too. After he recovered, Dad sought employment with benefits and a pension plan. As luck would have it, the county school system needed a maintenance crew to tend to the boilers, air conditioners, cafeteria equipment, lights, scoreboards, and, well, everything, so they hired a top-flight crew—they hired my dad.

Despite the struggle to escape poverty, the long hours, and the frequent serious injuries, Dad always loved life and lusted for laughter. He loved playing practical jokes aimed at his long-suffering children, our sainted and serious mother, and the entire school staff. If the man they fondly called "Doc" (the beloved Janitor) came up a bucket or a mop short and knew someone had hidden it to ruffle his feathers, Dad would find a sneaky, yet harmless way, to retaliate. Unaware teachers would futilely try to locate the source of the little pieces of wire that dropped into someone's hair as he or she walked under the gymnasium scoreboard.

At home, on any given Sunday, Mom would tell us a small, somber story, usually with a moral. Dad would sit quietly, fiddling with his teaspoon as he too listened. His impish eyes, however, would give him away. Shortly thereafter, Dad would aim the spoon, wait for Mom to reach the climax of her tale, and then, with a firm and calculated axe chop, send the spoon twirling into the air and crashing onto her plate. Mom would scold him, and Dad would sheepishly duck his head, place a hand over his mouth and snicker. We kids would roar with laughter.

That's my dad—a man of demonstrable character, charm, humor, and honor far beyond his most modest attainments. He didn't leap over tall buildings, but he always gave more of everything than he himself received. I won't tip my spoon, but I will tip my hat—here's to you, Dad. ❧

DENNIS C. BENTLEY works as an IT consultant in St. Louis, Missouri, and suffers for inheriting his father's damnable work ethic. The author's father, Sam Bentley, is retired and still living in, and making repairs to, the family home in Cerulean, Kentucky.

Year of the Schwinn

SUSAN SUNDWALL

We'd only been in California for three years when my tenth birthday was on the horizon. We were transplants from northern Minnesota back in the late 1950s, and Dad had worked hard to get us there. To make the money to fly us all out, he spent eight months in Greenland where the U.S. Army had contracted with civilians to build an airstrip. It was an exciting time for all of us because California seemed like a wonderland where just about anybody's dream could come true. Still, with five children to feed and clothe it was a struggle to make ends meet. Dad found one salesman's job after another and pounded the pavement selling screen doors, then vitamin supplements, then encyclopedias until finally he got a sales route for a meat-packing company. Even then the money often ran out before the month did. My mother didn't have an outside job and neither did she drive. This left a lot of responsibility on my dad who had to spend his off-hours shuttling us to doctor's appointments, school meetings, and grocery stores.

My birthday fell on a Saturday that year and I woke up wondering what the day would bring. No mention was made of anything special being done for my birthday so I imagined I'd get cards and small gifts like all my other birthdays. There was one thing I dreaded about the day, though. I had a morning appointment with the eye doctor. Yuck. I sure didn't want to go to that. Dad would be taking me, conferring with the doctor about my poor eyesight and whether I'd need new glasses or not. New glasses meant the kids at school would stare at me for a day or so and I hated that idea. But the hour came to go off for my exam and I had to go, grumbling about the unfairness of having this appointment on my birthday. During the trip to the eye doctor my Dad was quiet. We sped through downtown traffic and I stared glumly out the car window hoping the appointment wouldn't take too long. I pouted through the half-hour exam and quite honestly, I don't remember whether I needed new glasses or not. I was just glad to be out of there. When we got back to the car, my dad *finally* mentioned my birthday. "I think your mom has something special for your birthday today," he said.

I brightened immediately. "Really?"

"Didn't you want a new hairbrush set or something?"

My face fell. That wasn't what I wanted at all. My heart was set on a small crystal clock for my bedside table. They were all the rage, not too expensive, and I thought they were beautiful. "That would be okay," I said. A hairbrush seemed more in keeping with gifts my folks could afford so I resigned myself to another *poor kid* birthday.

"Well, we have to make a stop before we head for home," Dad said. "It won't take long."

A few minutes later, we pulled up in front of a bicycle shop where a long row of beautiful Schwinn bicycles lined the sidewalk in front of the store.

"Why are we stopping here?" I asked.

"Because you're getting a new bicycle for your birthday."

I stared at him, probably with my mouth open. I didn't believe him. I was the girl who pretended that things like new bicycles weren't important. I was the girl who begged to ride on the back of her girlfriend's bikes so I could be a part of the group that was heading for the playground after school. If nobody would give me a ride I walked or acted like I didn't really want to go anyway. I had so many defenses for why I didn't have things like roller skates, nice clothes, or fashion dolls that my mind refused to accept that this could change. And here was my wonderful Dad telling me I was getting a new bicycle for my tenth birthday. I just stared at him.

My Dad had the kind of grin that split his whole face and that's what happened when he saw my reaction. I think he already had the bike he could afford picked out because he led me to a beautiful dark green one and asked me how I liked it. Now, let me tell you, this bike was a magnificent monster. Not a lightweight like you find so much nowadays. It had substantial metal fenders, whitewall tires (with inner tubes), a chain guard, a sturdy kickstand, a basket on the front, and a bell on the handlebars, plus a rack on the back fender where another kid could ride. And the spokes! Imagine all the cards I could clothespin to those. My girlfriends would die of envy. Did I like it? I was simply too stunned to answer.

Dad loaded the bike and took it and his stunned oldest daughter home. He didn't stop grinning for weeks, and when I got over my disbelief at owning this beautiful object, I didn't either. Later, my Mom told me the bike cost $48, and in those days that was a lot of groceries. Whatever he had to do to afford my bike, Dad did it without complaint or boasting. Looking back, I realize he may have seen that purchase as a mile marker on the road to prosperity and been proud of it. But his pride could never have matched mine. I rode that bike into the ground and will never forget the joy and head-tossing pride I felt in being able to ride with my friends to the playground, haul my brothers and sisters around on the rack, and love the man to bits who allowed me to do it. Thanks Dad!

SUSAN SUNDWALL is a freelance writer and children's playwright. She works from her home in upstate New York and has just completed her first novel—a cozy mystery. Her play *Easter Lillian* is available from Standard Publishing.

When I moved into a basement apartment in Boston after graduation, my stepfather volunteered to help paint the dingy, gray walls to make the dark studio brighter. He also showed up unexpectedly with a new TV—my first. "I know you can't survive without one of these," he said. He was right.

One day, I accidentally locked myself in my basement apartment on my way to work. The doorknob had fallen off in my hand. The windows had bars on them. There was no way out until the landlord could return to release me. When I called home in a mild state of panic, my stepfather answered. "Don't worry. You'll be fine," he said.

I hung up and sat on my bed. The phone rang. "Don't smoke a cigarette and don't turn the stove on," my stepfather said firmly.

"Why?" I asked.

"I don't want you to start a fire and not be able to get out."

In the next few years, I moved to three more apartments. Somewhere among those moves, my stepfather became my Dads too. Maybe because he volunteered for the moving crew each time, maybe because I had finally surrendered my fantasies and accepted reality—Dads was a constant. He was always bringing me things: an old side table from a dump or yard sale that he had re-glued and painted to make it much more attractive and a print of an elephant—my favorite animal—that he framed. Each time he reminded me of how much crap—as he fondly called it—he would like me to move out of their house.

Somewhere during those moves, my father got divorced again.

I was thirty years old when I married. I had a Master's degree and a writing and teaching career. I didn't feel any man had the right to give me away to any other man. Nor could I choose between my fathers, so I walked down the narrow aisle of the country church by myself with my two fathers shoulder to shoulder behind me.

When my husband and I unpacked our wedding presents and furniture I asked him to carry a heavy Bloomingdales box from my mother and Dads into our apartment. I couldn't imagine what the gift inside could be. When I opened it, Dads' handiwork looked up at me. He had packed all the textbooks and papers I had never been able to throw out. This time I laughed with him.

My children were present at my father's fourth wedding.

Thirty-four years after they married, my mother was diagnosed with cancer. Dads and I teamed up to drive her to the doctor and to the chemotherapy appointments. When she died seven months later, Dads and I huddled in his study one dark night. "The best thing Mummy ever did was to marry you," I said quietly. He nodded and patted my hand.

These days, Dads attends his grandchildren's plays and sporting events, and plans family visits to his summerhouse. He's become very adept at buying tasteful Christmas and birthday presents. I hope he teaches my children how to change a tire.

MORGAN BAKER'S essays have been published in *The New York Times*, *The Boston Globe*, United Parenting Publications, and *The Martha's Vineyard Times*. She teaches creative nonfiction and magazine writing at Emerson College in Boston. She lives in Cambridge with her husband, two daughters, and two dogs.

The Greatest Dad Award Goes To …

SYLVIA BRIGHT-GREEN

Summertime on our 120-acre farm along the Rock River is my most memorable time of being with my dad. Probably because my brothers and sisters (fourteen of us) at varying times worked long and hard hours doing farm chores with dad lovingly at our side. And through all this dusk-until-dawn work, my dad joked, teased, and kept us laughing with his singing of "The Old Grey Mare, She Ain't What She Used to Be."

Our tedious, muscle-aching chores began at four in the morning and ended at sundown. Chores such as milking the cows, slopping the hogs, feeding the chickens, threshing, harvesting the corn, bringing in the hay, making silage, gathering eggs, canning all the garden bounty, and other numerous farm duties.

And no matter what we did or didn't do, Dad never once hit or yelled at us whenever we got out of control or made a mistake, because he believed in us being ourselves, and learning through our mistakes. But if we made that mistake more than once, Dad would give us one of his famous looks that said, "Do I have to take you behind the barn or in the woodshed?" His behind the barn or woodshed looks weren't what was generally meant, such as a thrashing, because Dad didn't believe in violence. What he meant was a tongue lashing, which could take anywhere up to an hour or more. And in that verbal lashing he would tell us how we were taught right from wrong, and how our mistakes made life harder for ourselves and others who had to fix them, and what purpose did it serve to do something if you're not going to do your best, and on and on and on with his commonsense ethics. Which could be worse at times than getting a thrashing. Especially when we kids had plans of going into town and "raising harmless cane" with our friends.

Don't get me wrong, just because Dad didn't believe in spanking, it didn't mean he was a pushover. He may have been a six-foot, Steven Segal–built type of farmer, tough on the outside and gentle on the inside—who could lift his weight in throwing bales of hay and pushing a John Deere tractor out of a muddy field—but he was also a caring, fair-minded man who gave everyone the benefit of the doubt, as he contended. He just didn't believe that using force or negativity served any purpose, when common sense and love served a better master.

My dad's common sense platitudes, through my growing and married years, came to mind many times when my life was darkened by fear and pain, and I lost my way. And it didn't matter whether it was just a small inconsequential happening like a scraped knee, or a life-altering event, such as a serious surgery, Dad's wisdom always found its way back to me.

My biggest life lesson with his wise counsel began when I was ten years old. It was on a hot summer afternoon, too hot to do anything but shade ourselves, and I was sitting on the porch steps of the farmhouse with tears running down my cheeks. Dad, noticing my discontent, asked, "Why aren't you playing in the tree house with your brothers?"

Through tears of rejection, I replied, "They don't want me to play with them because I don't know how to climb, and they wouldn't teach me. They also said they didn't want a 'stinky old girl' in their special place."

Taking my hand, Dad consolingly said, "Come, I'll help you make your own tree house and teach you how to climb."

Hand in hand, Dad and I walked, and as we walked, he said, "There are three things you need to know to survive as a girl in a boy's world. Things such as how to drive a car, bait a fishhook, and climb a tree. Knowing these things will also help to serve you in the adult world. For example: Being able to drive a car will give you independence; baiting a hook gives you the know-how to fish so that you will never go hungry; and being skilled at climbing a tree teaches you how to deal with life."

When we reached an old oak tree just a short distance inside the woods, not far from the house, we stopped. The tree was huge, not in stature, but in width. Dad then showed me how the knots on the tree could be used as steps enabling me to climb to the tree's highest branches.

"Climbing a tree isn't much different than learning how to mount every challenge you're going to encounter in life. Let's say that the tree is the obstacle you want to conquer," he explained.

"Gather your courage and move forth doing what you think is best, using what you have to work with. If you fail, keep trying, but always look for the positive in the learning."

At those tender years I didn't quite understand what he was saying. But I did discover at an early age, that when Dad said something—being a man who didn't mince words—I had better put them to memory. And while I was putting his words to memory, Dad added: "Whenever your chores are done, you can come to your special tree house and play. But bear in mind, that whatever you choose to do, in work or play, you do it from your heart, not your head," he emphasized. "Because the heart is absolute love and therein lies your true desires and happiness."

Through my growing years some of Dad's words became lost in the recesses of my mind. And remained so, until I was reminded of them when I most needed to recall them: first when my husband died, and later when my father died. Thank you, Dad, for sowing your seeds of wisdom in my young mind to use when I really needed to harvest them the most.

Therefore, the "Greatest Dad Award" goes to . . . Wilbur Cole Bright, my father.

SYLVIA BRIGHT-GREEN in her twenty-eight-year writing career has been published in five books, three by Adams Media, and has sold manuscripts to more than 700 newspapers and national magazines.

From Chicken Farmer to the Chicago Bears

ERIN FANNING

Many players in the National Football League ran faster, threw farther, and blocked harder than Stan Fanning. But during the 1961 season, my father earned his own superlative —the local media named him the Chicago Bears' "Biggest Bear." His statistics—6'7", 270 lbs.—seem almost puny by today's NFL lineup, but in 1961, when he swaggered onto the field and took his place as an offensive tackle, he was the biggest man in the game.

Dad had traveled a long distance from the small farm outside of Pullman, Washington, where he raised chickens to help pay for his expenses at the University of Idaho. But few who knew him would have been surprised—Dad had always attacked life with determination. "I've set my mind to making the team," he said in an article about his chicken farming and upcoming NFL career, written a few months before he headed off to the Bears' training camp.

He translated this intense drive into his own personal playbook—a combination of hard work, optimism, and courage—that took him from rural America to the NFL to a career in international sales. Early on, life threw him curve balls that could have thrown him off course, or at least turned him into a pessimist. Instead, my dad turned disasters into triumphs, and used them to strengthen his resolve to succeed.

"I never made state all-conference while in high school," he said in the same article, explaining some of the challenges he had faced in his football career. His choice of words was an understatement, so typical of Dad to downplay the hardships that stood in his path to the NFL.

He didn't mention the battle with dyslexia that had made schoolwork a constant struggle, or that a discouraging football coach had once proclaimed (loudly), "You'll never play in the pros." Dad didn't mention that his dream to play in the NFL dissolved during his final years of high school when Ken, one of his four younger brothers, the one closest to Dad's age, was diagnosed with cancer.

Dad didn't mention these things because he didn't believe in complaining, and he was stoic. I'm sure my dad didn't think a fluff piece was the right venue to discuss his brother's cancer, which had attacked Ken with an endless supply of artillery.

Ken eventually lost his leg to the disease, but when he returned to school, he resumed his duties as sophomore class president. Prior to the cancer, Ken had also been a state-ranked wrestler, but rather than feel bitter, he coped by becoming the wrestling team's manager and assistant coach.

My father decided to join the wrestling team—if his brother could no longer wrestle, Dad would become his legs. And he attacked it with his typical gusto. Between his motivation to play on his brother's behalf and his work ethic, Dad's wrestling career took on a meaning larger than the sport, and propelled him farther than a rookie wrestler deserved to go. With Ken on the sidelines, Dad tackled local tournaments, then district matches, and finally state contests. In each, he drilled down the competition, eventually winning second place in the Washington state championships. Ken stood next to Dad on the podium, sharing what my father would have seen as their mutual success.

And behind all this—struggling with school, dreaming about the NFL, and watching his younger brother battle with a fatal illness—my dad always had a long list of farm chores and chickens to tend. In the photograph that accompanies the article, Dad held up a football in one hand and an egg in the other. Black-framed glasses perched on his nose, giving him the look of Clark Kent—his Superman persona hidden until unleashed on the football field. In the photograph, Dad grinned, his chin jutted out, as if he were already marching forward to meet his dreams.

Dad played professional football for about five years, but after his first year, he rarely started. He played for the Denver Broncos briefly, and then ended his short career with the Los Angeles Rams. He may not have fulfilled all his NFL hopes, but in typical Dad fashion, he moved on with enthusiasm—traveling the world and throwing his energy into downhill skiing and bicycle touring.

Most importantly, though, he won big as a father. He developed his own playbook for life, teaching courage and optimism through his example. He might have earned the title "Biggest Bear" for only one season, but he remained so for me the rest of his life, not only in size but also in deed.

ERIN FANNING splits her time between the mountains of central Idaho and the lakes of northern Michigan. She's the author of *Mountain Biking Michigan* (Globe Pequot Press) and writes for magazines like *Quiet Sports, Oregon Outside, RV Life,* and *American Profile.*

Kite Lessons

KIM KLUGH

The thin, white string unraveled in my father's hand as he launched the kite, which fluttered and flapped against the spring gusts. A surge of power took hold whenever Dad handed me the stick he'd fashioned into a spool for the twine, and the whimsical kite would then be in my control. It was a job keeping the line taut and the kite aloft. It came down to learning how to simultaneously hold on while letting go, depending on the air currents. Unexpectedly, the kite caught an updraft and twirled frenetically or whipped around, tugging the anchor in my hands. At times it seemed almost lifelike as it swirled and chased its tail, then plummeted and crashed to the ground.

Sometimes Dad wrote notes on scraps of paper tucked into his pockets and secretly attached them to the string. They too flew up into the blue and the clouds and flapped wildly against the twine. When the wind died down and the kite finally came to rest somewhere else in the yard or the adjoining cornfields, my siblings and I raced to read the silly messages which Dad dubbed "kite mail." Would they promise piggyback rides or ice cream after dinner? We never knew until we pounced upon the downed kite, tore off the paper scrap and read it aloud. Dad's hastily scribed airborne notes added a hint of mystery to even the simple act of kite flying.

As spring unfolded and warm breezes wafted, we danced into summertime. School was out and bedtimes were extended. We flitted in the twilight like sprites until fireflies filled our yard, and then we filled our glass jelly jars with the iridescent creatures. Dad took his hammer and a small nail from the back cellar workbench and with weathered hands punched holes into the metal lids so the frantic insects could breathe. We watched their soft flickering against the glass, and then Dad prompted us to release the flashing bugs back into the thick summer air.

On countless summer evenings when time seemed to stand still, Dad called to us above the roar of the mower, "Get your bats and gloves and meet me in the side yard as soon as I'm finished mowing the lawn!" There he pitched to us until we successfully hit the ball and got on base. We dashed at the crack of the bat; he fielded the ball and sprinted to tag us, and sometimes lifted us up and carried us across the yard. Mom watched from the sidelines on a lawn chair, happy to have the excuse to sit after a tiring day, or cheered from inside as she leaned on the sill of a bedroom window until it grew too dark to see the ball.

However, that didn't stop my dad from play; he called to Mom to turn on the bright outdoor lights that lit up our side yard, much like a major league stadium, or so we thought. We continued play until the grass grew too slippery with the evening dew, and we finally had to call it a game before Mom called to Dad, "Cliff, someone's going to get hurt and it'll probably be you!"

On lazy Sunday afternoons when autumn's breath began to feel more like winter, after church and before supper, we either set up the card table or found cozy spots on the floor in front of the fireplace and played a wide assortment of games. Striped peppermint canes, peanut brittle, a gingerbread man, gumdrops, lollipops, and a Neapolitan ice cream brick made our mouths water when we played Candyland. Frustrations mounted over the consequences of good and bad deeds in Chutes and Ladders, and the multicolored body parts and appendages of Cootie, the silly plastic bug, always fell out of their appointed holes.

As our attention spans lengthened and our interests broadened, Dad took down more advanced games from the closet shelf. There were rounds of Parcheesi, tournaments of checkers, vocabulary building Anagrams and Spill and Spell, and the fast-flying numbers on Flinch cards. Then there was finally the day Dad brought out the favorite games of his youth—Scrabble and Monopoly. We knew we had moved up more than a notch in game playing ability when Dad introduced those games. "Play to the end" and "no cheating whatsoever" were the indisputable rules—good sportsmanship was a given in our household.

In the winter when the country roads were impassable and even board games and jigsaw puzzles couldn't banish our feelings of confinement, our own Lampeter Road beckoned my father. Out of storage came the trusty Flexible Flyer sled. Out we went, waddling like chubby snowmen in our winter layers, into the frosty night and onto the snow-coated road to go sledding. Dad gave us running pushes and then gently leapt on too. We soared, three-pile high, down the road into the snowy darkness laughing and screeching in wild abandon. After all sensation left our fingers and toes, we reluctantly tramped back to the house, shed our outer trappings and wrapped our hands around steamy mugs of hot cocoa, loaded with spongy, bobbing marshmallows.

Years later Dad shifted gears on the company truck for the last time. His arthritic knees took the brunt of the impact as he hoisted his body out of the driver's seat and headed for a life of retirement. I doubt my father was aware of the collective legacy he was creating as he herded us through childhood. I've since inherited Scrabble and Monopoly, while the checkerboard went to my brother and Flinch cards to my sister. Various grandchildren have practiced spelling skills with the Spill and Spell game when visiting Grandpa. The Flexible Flyer's coasted across many an ice-coated hillside—this time with me piling on top of my children. I still watch for the arrival of the season's first firefly and scribble silly notes on Post-its to my own children.

I'm now the parent attempting to keep the proverbial kite aloft. I'm feeling my children tug and pull at their anchors; they long for the current that will take them soaring and floating beyond my reach. I don't want to let go of the connecting line, neither do I want it to snap, so I begin to let go in intervals, giving it some slack, but not quite giving it up. I'm on the ground watching them flutter and sail and sometimes dive and crash. Like Dad, I'm gradually unraveling the twine, simultaneously trying to hold on while letting go. ❧

KIM KLUGH, whose adult children fly their own kites these days, immerses herself in teenage angst by lending academic support to high school students at her day job. After the final bell rings for the school day, she dashes home (to husband and pets) and works on freelance assignments for a business publication geared toward women. She's enjoyed the thrill of seeing her byline appear in regional magazines and lifestyle articles for her hometown newspaper.

When No One Was Watching

SUSAN BREEDEN

The living room curtains were open and, just beyond the glass, a willow tree's delicate limbs shivered against the slightest breeze. Canadian fronts usually didn't forge a path that stretched down to the Texas Gulf Coast city of Lake Jackson, but this one had ridden my bumper all the way home from the University of Texas campus in Austin the evening before.

The sun had yet to rise, but my father was already awake. In the kitchen, our cat devoured the feast spread out before her, my father having given the feline more choices than one would find at a Chinese lunch buffet. He had also prepared the coffee-maker, even though he didn't drink the stuff. The smell of freshly scooped grounds still lingered in the air. As always, he had placed my favorite coffee mug within arm's length, alongside a packet of sweetener, a crystal creamer filled with half-and-half, and a silver spoon. The only effort required of me was the flip of a switch.

I opened the side door and stuck my head outside. That's where I found him, barefooted, wearing a thin T-shirt and stained khakis. He sat on the cold cement next to a wheel of my Chevy Malibu, scrubbing the white wall with a toothbrush and leaning in to examine his handiwork with the intensity of focus that Michelangelo might have given *David*.

"You don't have to do that, Daddy."

"They look so much better when they're clean," he said, surprised by my voice but not the least bit dissuaded. He resumed work on his masterpiece. I went back inside where it was warm. A few minutes later, he rushed in at his usual brisk pace. Any faster and the man would have been sprinting.

"Where are your keys? One of the back tires needs some air," he said.

"I can take care of that later." I'd barely touched my first cup of coffee so my internal engine hadn't warmed up yet. His, however, was already in high gear.

He dismissed my suggestion with a wave of a hand. "Might as well get it out of the way."

My keys lay on the harvest table, right where I left them. He patted his back pocket to make sure his wallet was there, then slipped his bare feet into some old brown loafers and sped out the side door. No use trying to talk him out of it, even if I could have caught up with him.

When my father made up his mind to be helpful, there was no stopping him. Especially when he was up before dawn. But broad daylight didn't slow him down either. Later that day I caught him, red-handed, sitting on the dining room floor with my boot in one hand and a polishing rag in the other. Our Michelangelo was at it again.

"Daddy, you don't have to do that," I said, echoing the same futile refrain.

"The heels are a little scuffed," he insisted.

If I had assumed his thoughtfulness ended there, I would have been mistaken. While heading back to Austin that Sunday afternoon, I noticed that my car had a full tank of gas.

My father always found ways to do such favors behind my back. And it wasn't as if he didn't have other responsibilities. He worked at the same company for over forty-two years. Until he needed back surgery just before he retired, he maintained a stellar attendance record. He never missed an opportunity to take on extra tasks and responsibilities at work or at church. All the while, he never missed a chance to take extra care of me, even when I was no longer a child. Even though he was always more than generous with his money, he taught me, through his actions, that the most special gifts are those that can't be bought. He demonstrated how integrity is measured by what a person gives in terms of time and thoughtfulness, and not by how much is earned or spent.

I finally married at the age of forty-three in Sedona, Arizona, with an open field as my sanctuary and the red rocks as the backdrop. My mother and father were the only witnesses, aside from the minister and photographer. After the groom and I said our vows and sealed our fate with a kiss, I needed a moment, away from our small gathering, to contemplate my new role in life. In a way, I was thankful that I didn't have a traditional wedding.

Otherwise, my father would have been required to give me away. Still, everything had changed, hadn't it?

As the sun began its descent behind nature's crimson sculpture, the temperature also dropped. Before I even so much as shivered, someone draped a suit jacket around my shoulders.

"Do that again," the photographer called out.

My father reluctantly agreed to repeat the motion. I eagerly complied. But most of all, I felt reassured to know that, even though I was now someone's wife, I was still Daddy's little girl.

I removed the jacket. My father held it just above my shoulders, as instructed. He seemed uncomfortable and awkward, being asked to stage an action that had come so naturally.

At that moment I realized how, once again, he had waited for a time when no one was watching to be a hero: specifically, my hero. Knowing my father, it won't be the last time.

SUSAN BREEDEN lives in Houston, Texas, and works as a technical editor. In her spare time, she writes commercial and literary fiction. When she isn't editing or writing, Susan enjoys spending time with her husband, or being pampered at her parents' home in Lake Jackson.

Grandpa's 'Possum

DOYLE SUIT

A marauding opossum searching for a midnight snack woke Edmon and Elizabeth Adams from a sound sleep. The chickens protested when the thief entered their house. Wearing only his nightshirt and hastily donned shoes, Ed grabbed his .22 rifle and ran to check on the racket. Chickens and their eggs provided food for the family, and he wasn't likely to share with varmints.

Elizabeth lay awake awaiting his return. She heard a rifle shot, and moments later, a second shot. Frightened, she scrambled from bed and ran to him. Ed was too thrifty with bullets to shoot twice. Something had to be wrong.

She found the dead 'possum, and she found Ed lying on the cold March earth stricken by a massive heart attack.

His last words were "Love you, Lizzie."

~

Six years earlier, during the summer of 1944, my father left my mother and five little boys on Grandpa's doorstep. I was the oldest—age ten. He also sold everything we owned, took the money, and disappeared from our lives.

The old couple had already raised ten children. Eight survived to become adults. Four sons served as military officers during the big war, and all their children had finally left home. Grandpa took us in and provided food and shelter we needed to survive. I still remember the smell of dried fruit and fresh-baked bread mingled with wood smoke in Grandma's kitchen.

It was my lot to help Grandpa with chores on the eighty-acre farm where he raised crops and ran cattle on open range. He was a thoughtful—sometimes impatient—teacher. I received a lesson on coping with a demanding world soon after we arrived.

A pasture gate had decayed. Grandpa replaced the rotted boards with irregular sawmill slabs, and we spent a morning patching the old gate. The work became tedious under the hot sun, and I convinced myself this was not the right way to run a farm.

"Grandpa," I said. "Why don't we buy a new gate and spend our time doing something to make money?"

The old man chuckled. "This farm doesn't run on income. It runs on lack of outgo."

Grandpa taught me to handle the horses and plow a straight furrow. He taught me to use the horse-drawn mower and buck rake before I turned eleven. His watchful eye monitored my use of an axe and saw to fell trees.

During the fall, we harvested a surplus of potatoes. A neighbor wanted to buy several bushels and offered a low price. He and Grandpa dickered for a half-hour before reaching an agreement. He paid for the potatoes, and Grandpa promised to deliver them the next day. I filled each basket level with its top.

Grandpa checked my work. "You need to add more potatoes to round them off."

"The basket holds a bushel when it's level full," I said. "He didn't pay for extra potatoes."

"It's okay to bargain for a good price when you sell something," he said. "But make sure to give a little extra when you deliver."

When a few of the range cattle failed to come home for salt, Grandpa saddled the horses. Heat, flies, saw-briars, second-growth brush, and rain took turns plaguing us while we rode the rough country to find them. We searched for the cows until we knew they were safe, and I learned about perseverance.

Grandpa had been eleven when his father died. He took a job in a sawmill to support the family and caught his left hand in the saw, losing parts of three fingers. Later, he taught himself to play the violin, pressing the strings with the stumps of fingers.

He completed only two years of formal schooling, but educated himself, passed state examinations, and taught school for twenty years. They had no access to a high school where he lived, so when the time came, Grandpa rented a house twenty-five miles away during the school term to educate his children.

He possessed considerable skill as a practical veterinarian for his farm animals, and some skill at patching up people in an area where doctors weren't handy. When I dislocated my shoulder, he snapped it back in place and put me in a sling for three days. A week later, I was good as new.

Grandpa's evil-tempered black horse carried him to church each Sunday. Nobody else could get along with the animal. Grandpa arrived early to build a fire and make sure the building was clean. He taught adult bible class and served as the stand-in preacher and song leader. I learned to sing at church, and he encouraged me to play the guitar.

Squirrels made a tasty treat, and most boys started hunting by age ten. Not me. I had to wait until I was twelve. Then Grandpa taught me to shoot the rifle and took me squirrel hunting. I missed my first shot.

"Take time to aim," he said. "If you're not sure you can hit him, don't pull the trigger. Bullets cost money."

Later—after I'd been successful in shooting a few squirrels—he added more advice. "If you shoot them in the head, you won't ruin any of the meat."

Grandpa was a stern and unyielding taskmaster, but his sense of humor showed on occasion. He taught me, "Hindsight is better than foresight by a darn sight."

We failed to agree on some things. He didn't approve of dancing, and—when I started high school—I'd slip off to attend a neighborhood dance on Saturday night. I think he knew, but he didn't say anything. I felt guilty anyway.

Baseball was even more contentious. The community sponsored an amateur baseball team, and—since I had dreams of playing for the St. Louis Cardinals someday—I wanted to play center field.

Grandpa had other priorities. "They play games on Sunday. Your time would be better spent keeping the Sabbath." I didn't give up easily, but I didn't play Sunday baseball, and I wasn't invited to try out for the Cardinals.

Grandpa was nearing seventy years old when he took us in, but I never heard him complain that we were a burden. I missed having a father growing up, but Grandpa was there for me. I haven't forgotten the example he set and the lessons he taught.

More than sixty years have flown by since Grandpa took me under his wing and showed me how he lived his faith. I'm blessed with a loving wife, stories to write, songs to sing, and grandkids that need an occasional nudge in the right direction. When my time comes, I hope I'm able to "kill my 'possum" before I leave this earth.

"Love you, Grandpa." ❧

DOYLE SUIT and his wife of a half-century live in St. Charles, Missouri, near their children and grandchildren. They dance, play golf and bridge, travel, and Doyle plays bluegrass music for fun. His work has appeared in *The St. Louis Suburban Journals, Good Old Days Magazine, Storyteller Magazine, Spring Hill Review, Sweetgum Notes, The Cuivre River Anthologies,* and other publications.

Daddy versus the
Golden Gate Bridge

SUSAN B. TOWNSEND

When I was about five years old, my father decided to return to university for his graduate degree. He chose the University of California at Berkeley, and since we lived in Edmonton, Alberta, his decision meant a significant adjustment in our lives. After renting our house, my parents loaded up the Volkswagen, squeezed my older brother and I into the backseat, and made the three-day drive to Berkeley. I had never been more than a few hundred miles away from Edmonton, and I was filled with excitement at the beginning of what I saw as a big adventure in a strange new place.

Our home for the next year was a tiny apartment in a building once used as army barracks during the Second World War. Rent for this deluxe accommodation was fifty dollars a month. This was a huge expense for my parents in view of the fact that there would be no income while my father attended university. The apartment was sordid and small. My mother spent the first night in tears after meeting our new roommates, huge cockroaches that raced for cover when the lights were turned on. She cleaned for what seemed like days before we were even allowed to unpack. Facing our building was another building exactly like it, and between the two was a huge common area planted with grass. We were living in the married students' quarters and there were children everywhere. Friendships were formed overnight, and there was always someone with whom to play. I started kindergarten, and although I spent an inordinate amount of time in the "chatterbox corner," life was good.

I saw little of my father during the week, but every Sunday the four of us would pile into the Volkswagen and drive to San Francisco. For a little girl from the prairies, San Francisco was an amazing and exotic place full of hills that climbed to the sky, cable cars and people of all shapes, sizes, and colors. It was there that I had my first look at the ocean. As I stared across the immense body of water, my father told me that from where we stood, the next stop would be Japan. I shook my head in disbelief. I believed in Santa Claus and the tooth fairy but I could not believe that an ocean could be that big.

Our Sundays in the city were usually spent at Golden Gate Park. One weekend, my father made the wonderful announcement that we were going to walk across the Golden Gate Bridge. My mother would drive across the bridge and wait for us on the other side. My enthusiasm for this latest adventure waned, as my short legs grew increasingly tired.

I continued my weary trudge and, then, I heard someone shout that a submarine was approaching. Everyone stopped and watched as the huge vessel began to make its way under the bridge. People were talking and pointing; many were standing on the ledge of the railing and leaning over for a better view. I couldn't see a thing. I tried stepping up to the edge of the railing to lean over as I saw others doing, but my father laid a firm hand on my shoulder and said, "No, you stay right where you are."

How frustrating! I was going to miss the fun if I didn't think of something. Without a moment's hesitation, I stuck my head between the bars of the bridge railings with very satisfying results. I had a perfect view. Within a few minutes, the flurry of excitement was over, and the submarine disappeared from sight.

It was then that my father noticed the position I had assumed in order to witness the spectacle. Unaware that my head was on the outside of the railing, he took me by the arm and tried to pull me to my feet. I screeched in pain. "Ow, ow, stop. I'm stuck."

My brother began to laugh. "What a dope. She's got her head stuck in the bridge."

His words threw me into a panic and I began to cry. My sobs turned into a howl. "Help me Daddy. I'm stuck. Help me, help me." People stopped to watch the new source of entertainment, and I heard a voice behind me. "That little girl is stuck in the bridge."

I'm sure my father must have wondered what the heck he was going to tell my mother. After ordering my brother to be quiet, my father knelt down beside me. "Don't worry sweetheart. I'll get you out." His words were calming, but not convincing. My struggling stopped, but my crying, accompanied by abundant hiccups and sniffles persisted. My father's soothing words continued, and my panic began to subside. "If you got your head in there," he reasoned, "you can get your head out of there." This made sense to me and I decided to try. Much to everyone's relief, my head came out as easily as it went in. With a feeling of triumph, I turned to my father with a huge grin on my puffy, tear-streaked face.

Many years later, my father attended an education conference in San Francisco. During his absence, I received a postcard of the Golden Gate Bridge. A circle was drawn around a section of the railings. An arrow pointed to the circle, and in my father's printing were the words, "Remember this?" The postcard is in a drawer somewhere but the memory of that day—and my father's gentle soul—will always be with me.

SUSAN B. TOWNSEND is a writer and stay-at-home mother who lives in Virginia with her husband and five children. She is the author of *A Bouquet for Mother* and *A Bouquet for Grandmother* and is the coeditor of several Christian volumes in the *Cup of Comfort*® series.

Riding with Santa Claus

DONNA MATTHEWS

The most interesting part of every day was the late afternoon when Dad made the veterinary visits that Mom referred to as "rounds" all over the neighborhood to check on someone's sick livestock or to assist with a delivery, trim hooves, or vaccinate an animal. I always made sure that I stayed close when it was time to go so I wouldn't get left behind. I enjoyed the time spent with Dad and the people and animals he visited. I got to see the first new lambs of spring and often came home with a new baby lamb riding on my lap, not to mention puppies, baby ducks, chicks, and lots of kittens. Dad had a quiet nature, strength and determination that allowed him to handle the most unruly animal and I learned many things by watching him from the top rail of stalls and corrals. I learned to read by reading the medicine bottles he sent me to get and became adept at retrieving things for him quickly and quietly without alarming the animal he was working on.

Rounds on Christmas Eve were different; they started right after morning chores and they were the ones I never wanted to miss. Mom had been baking and cooking for days in preparation for the holidays and today she had several cardboard boxes lined up on the kitchen table filled with an assortment of goodies. While I struggled into my snowsuit and tried hard to remember how to tell which boot went on which foot, Dad and Mom loaded the back seat and trunk of the car with the boxes.

We stopped first at the Hockett's house, to visit the elderly couple who only had a dog. Their house had one main room that was heated by a barrel stove in one corner and a cast iron cook stove on the other end. Mr. Hockett opened the front door and waved us in when he saw us drive into the yard. Dad helped me out of the car and grabbed one of the boxes as he yelled a greeting to Mr. Hockett. The house was warm and old Butch, the Border collie, stretched and got up from his rug in front of the barrel stove and came to meet us. Dad bent down and checked his eyes as Mrs. Hockett started unpacking the box while giving us a rambling commentary on the weather, the neighborhood, and how much I had grown. There was a gallon of milk, a duck for their Christmas dinner, a bag of potatoes and onions, a dozen eggs, cookies, jelly, butter and a loaf of bread fresh from the oven wrapped in a new dishtowel made from a flour sack. Neither of the Hocketts could hear very well, nor did they get much company, so they both talked at the same time, loudly and on different subjects. Mrs. Hockett put steaming mugs of coffee in front of the men and hot chocolate in front of me, talking all the while. Dad drank his coffee, managing to participate in both conversations and be heard. When he had finished, he thanked them, wished them a merry Christmas, and we set out for Little Ted's.

Ted was a bachelor that lived down a rutted winding trail back in the woods. Naturally short by stature, a fall from the second story of a barn while loading hay left him with a broken back and a stooped-over shuffling gait. His one-room house was sided with tarpaper and took a huge supply of wood to keep it heated. He kept a few dairy cows in a barn behind the house. His habit of partaking in the bottled spirits made him one of the regulars on Dad's daily route. Dad made sure that the cattle had feed and water and care in the event that Ted wasn't up to remembering that he had them.

This morning Ted was in the yard chopping wood when we drove in. He greeted us with a big wave and yelled, "C'mon' in, coffee's on." We followed him into the dark kitchen where his blackened coffeepot stood on the wood cook stove perpetually boiling. When the need arose, he just added more water and grounds until the pot became so full of grounds that he had to dump it and start over. At Ted's I got to drink coffee too, with lots of sugar. Dad sat the box on the table as Ted filled mugs with the thick black liquid and they talked about how the cows were doing. Ted took a big spoon and dumped three heaping scoops of sugar into my coffee and gave me the spoon to stir it. I stirred and sipped it from the spoon listening to Dad ask about Ted's hay supply, knowing that I would get to come along when Dad hitched the draft horses to the bobsled and brought him a load of hay and wood. When we got up to leave, Ted thanked us and then reached back into the cupboard and pulled out a candy dish that his mother had brought with her from Holland. He wiped the dust out of it with his shirttail and handed it to me and said, "Merry Christmas."

At the Schmidt's, I was delighted to see Sadie, the Belgian mare, outside in the corral by the barn. The sun glistened off her coppery red coat and her breath was warm on my face as she reached over the fence to nuzzle my cheek. Last fall she had gotten caught in some stray barbed wire and cut her leg badly. Both Grandma and Grandpa Schmidt watched Dad care for her every day with tears in their eyes. Gentle Sadie stood quietly and bravely through it all and was as good as new now. Reluctantly, I left Sadie to join Dad as he went into the house. We left the box and continued on with new mittens and socks that Grandma Schmidt had knitted.

It was dark before we had delivered all of the boxes and Dad turned the old car for home. I drifted off to sleep with memories of the love and smiles I had seen all day. I dreamt that I was riding with Santa Claus.

DONNA MATTHEWS was raised in the cow pastures of Minnesota. She writes stories of reflections on life lessons learned from following her father on his rounds for a monthly newsletter for farmers and ranchers.

There and Back Again with Daddy

EVA MELISSA BARNETT

N o matter how many times Daddy watched me sing, he always made sure he was in the front row. I'd step on stage, stomach aflutter, and find him. The spotlights reflecting off his glasses served as his signal, a secret message to me: "Here I am, sweetie. Enjoy the moment." From then on it felt like it was just Daddy and me in that hot, musty auditorium. I felt calm and could sing, my voice strong and smooth. It wasn't just my performances, Daddy made sure he was in the front row in life too, seeking adventures to share with our family. By the time I was thirteen we'd visited every California mission; seen famous dams, bridges, and buildings; stood at the graves of history's most important men; and stopped to read every dusty plaque along the way.

For each family trip there were at least twice as many books scattered across the shelves and tables at home. After he'd finished his newspaper and I returned from rehearsal, there were pages of adventures we experienced from our lumpy sofa. More than once we trekked through the Misty Mountains with Bilbo and the dwarves. Occasionally he'd make up his own comical dialogue to see if I was still listening. I was.

But it wasn't enough just to see places and read about adventures. Daddy was always finding ways to live history. While my friends' fathers ate chips during the football game, Daddy made chain mail and shields. His crest: three dragons for his three daughters whose elementary school mascot was the dragon. We'd try on his clinking tunic and watch as the metal links fell to the floor, almost too heavy to let us stand upright. He'd smile and hand us his homemade sword too.

After his medieval phase, he took up Civil War re-enacting. This time, instead of trying on his uniform, Daddy took me to a tailor and had a dress fitted. He gave me a book to learn things like why sleeves weren't attached (for easier care and washing) and why plaids and small prints were popular (to allow the fabric to be turned inside out and used again after one side became worn).

Once I learned all I could in my own living room, it was off to a ball to waltz and make our way through a true Virginia reel. It didn't matter that the room was crowded or that everyone else was waltzing more slowly. He'd spin me as fast as he could, in and through everyone, by the band, by the seats, there and back again, until the songs ended and we remembered to catch our breaths. It was then I realized my daddy didn't just love history; he loved making history together.

Before I graduated from high school, Daddy wanted to share one more adventure, a river-rafting trip. I braided my hair to keep it off my face, while he gobbed sun block around his ears, leaving traces in his thick sideburns. The water was frigid, raising goose bumps along my arms and legs. Still, on the milder rapids, we'd jump in the water and float beside the raft.

"Remember to keep your head up and watch your feet," he'd say. "You never know what debris might be hidden in the water." I'd nod, enjoying the rush, my glittery toenails bobbing in front of me.

The rougher rapids were wild. Over the crashing water, we'd hear the guide shout instructions, "Back paddle left! Front paddle right!" I'd see Daddy's crazy grin as he maneuvered his oar, eyes squinting under the brim of his cap through the sun and spray. Sometimes it was all we could do to hold on to our oars, chilly foam washing over our laps.

But some rapids were dangerous, like "Satan's Cesspool." For that, the guide instructed us to simply hold on as he steered our raft through to calmer waters. I kept my head down and feet tucked tight into the safety slots of the raft. After we were through I looked up and saw Daddy watching me, making sure I was safe. Suddenly, it was just us again in that big canyon of blue sky and red stone.

These days the spotlight has shifted to my two babies. My son is so young he requires constant care and my daughter doesn't like my singing, unless she's requesting the animals for Old MacDonald's farm. The only adventures Daddy and I share are long-distance. He sits in his wheelchair, a cancerous disease having aged him prematurely. His speech is slow and his hands tremble, but he's still living life in the front row.

Just recently, my week had been stressful, tiring, much too long, and it was only Tuesday. The messy house seemed ready to swallow me, and I longed for some beacon of light to cut through my dreariness. Or better yet, beam me up and away. I called Daddy.

Taking him through my burdens like some nightmarish tour, he listened like only a father can, then spoke carefully. "Remember that river-rafting trip we took when you were in high school?" he asked.

"Yes," I answered, thinking about how I'd drifted under that robin's egg sky, without a care in the world.

"Well, parts of that ride we enjoyed and other parts, we just had to hold on. I think life's like that. And I think right now, you might be in a part of the ride where you just need to hold on."

I closed my teary eyes and nodded.

"But don't worry, sweetie. You'll get to enjoy it again."

Even with the crackling phone connection and the miles between us, it felt like he was sitting front and center, applauding my effort. As always, I gained new confidence in my most important performance yet, as a mother.

I want to give my children the childhood he gave me, full of stories, dances, nature, and gratitude. Looking at my son helps me remember that. He's named after my Daddy.

By definition, my father is now "disabled." I've never known a more misleading term. He is my front-row fan, my teacher, my reading buddy, my adventure-sharer, my history-maker, my inspiration when I'm afraid to take another step. He steps bravely into each day with bright eyes and a hopeful heart. ✒

EVA MELISSA BARNETT is an award-winning writer and songwriter from Davis, California. She loves long road trips, reading to her children, and attending Civil War balls with her sweet husband. Visit her blog for more reflections on the wonderful mishaps that make up life at *www .evamelissabarnett.blogspot.com.*

Daddy and the Dodgers

TERRI ELDERS

God gives every bird his worm, but he does not throw it into the nest.—Swedish proverb

Daddy never minced words when it came to his beloved Brooklyn Dodgers. The old Ebbets Field fans' mantra of hope, "Wait until next year," never crossed his lips. "Those damn Dodgers," he'd growl instead. "They deserved to lose. They threw the game away. You've gotta earn the victory. It doesn't just get handed to you." He espoused an equally no-nonsense approach to child rearing. After he and Mama adopted my sister and me in 1942, whenever we would visit Newberry's or Woolworth's and plead for a new toy, Daddy would quote the slogan, "Use it all, wear it out, make it do, or do without." Daddy could have written that World War II motto himself. "You each already have a doll," he would say, shaking his head at what he viewed as our grandiose expectations. Mama tried to make up for it, spending long December evenings ripping up our outgrown blouses and nightgowns to make doll clothes, hoping to counter any Christmas morning disappointment.

Raised in Kansas, the son of a prison guard and a mother who would later become the president of the Los Angeles chapter of the Women's Christian Temperance Union, Daddy frowned on frills. Because he worked two jobs, as a diesel mechanic by day, and a shoe salesman on Friday night and Saturday, he had little spare time. He and Mama traditionally spent Saturday nights together, visiting friends for a pinochle game. That left just a few weeknights and Sundays for family activities.

By the time I started junior high in 1948, I used to beg Daddy to take us all to the Sunday matinee. All my friends had gone with their families to see *The Red Shoes* or *Portrait of Jennie*. "Just listen to the radio," he'd say. "It's free and good enough." So instead of heading for the Temple or the Rialto, we'd chuckle along with studio audiences at *The Jack Benny Show*.

When Benny got the biggest laugh ever registered on radio by replying, "I'm thinking it over," when a mugger demanded, "Your money or your life," Mama said that sounded just like Daddy. Daddy scowled at first, but then nodded, as if these were words of praise. Mama also used to joke that when Daddy opened his wallet, moths would fly out. Daddy would counter that he was frugal, not stingy; thrifty, not a spendthrift. But he turned his back to us when he opened his wallet to fish out some change, as if to hide his stash from prying eyes.

The Dodgers were his one indulgence. Whenever the reception from the east coast was strong enough, Daddy hunkered down in front of the Philco, munching on a peanut butter sandwich, scribbling on a sheet of paper he called a scorecard. Seeking a way to get his attention, I, too, became a fan. I checked out stacks of library books to learn about the infield fly rule and why triple plays are so rare.

In the late afternoon I would hover by the front porch, watching for the *Herald Express* paperboy so I could follow the daily recounts of the Dodgers' battles. Though Daddy and I admired Jackie Robinson, we especially cheered when Duke Snider, deemed the Duke of Flatbush but actually a native Angeleno, hammered in another homer.

Soon we expanded our fandom to the Pacific Coast League Hollywood Stars, as well, and doubled our evening listening time, tuning out complaints from Mama and my sister about missing *Your Hit Parade* and *Lux Radio Theater*. When we weren't nodding our heads in approval over the feats of outfielder Frankie Kelleher, Daddy would help me with my geometry homework. "I don't know why they make girls take this stuff," he'd say, as I struggled with lengths, areas, and volumes. "It's not as if you're going to be an engineer."

"But, Daddy, I need to understand math if I'm to figure out the baseball odds and understand the stats."

"Well, that's certainly true," he conceded.

Once I started high school, I began a series of evening and Saturday jobs as a waitress, a sales clerk at a hosiery counter, and a bus girl, so could no longer join Daddy in listening to the games. By then we had a second radio—and even a television. And my interests had expanded beyond baseball, mostly to boys.

So when Daddy asked me to accompany him to Gilmore Field one Sunday to watch the Stars play a double-header against their archrivals, the Los Angeles Angels, I was both astonished and ambivalent. Sundays I usually went to the bowling alley or the miniature golf course with my boyfriend. On the other hand, Daddy had never asked me to go anywhere with him before. I hesitated only a second before accepting.

That Sunday game turned out to be one that became infamous as "The Brawl." The popular and usually mild-mannered Kelleher took an Angel pitch to his back after a pair of close brush-backs, strode out to the mound, and threw a punch, setting off a violent brawl that lasted over half an hour and required fifty police officers to break it up and restore order. A second donnybrook erupted a little later. And that was only the first game of a double-header.

I spilled my popcorn when I jumped up to cheer when Kelleher decked the pitcher, but Daddy told me to sit down and refused to buy me a second bag. And when I wanted to stay for the second game, Daddy shook his head in disgust. "It's bad enough that the players behaved like hooligans," he said, "but the audience endorsing it makes it worse. And that includes you, young lady."

On the long drive back from Hollywood to southwest Los Angeles, Daddy asked, "What if the Dodgers behaved like that? What if they had spilled off the bench and ambushed Bobby Thompson when he hit that homer off Branca back in '51? Would you have cheered just because they were Dodgers?"

"No," I said, "But that's different. Thompson hit 'the shot heard round the world.' Kelleher got hit by a ball."

"How do you know Hatten hit him on purpose? Didn't look like that to me."

Daddy shot me a sideways glance. "Terri, one thing you have got to remember, both in sports and life. You have to earn everything fair and square. It's not fair to take advantage of somebody else's mistakes. The better team should win. The better player should prevail. And hard work will pay off, not cheap tricks. There's no room in baseball for brawls."

"Well, the Stars did win. So I guess they're the better team."

Daddy shook his head and drove the rest of the way home in stony silence.

A few nights later I tuned in the Stars game. "Turn it off," Daddy ordered. "I'm through with those guys. And they call the Dodgers 'bums'! That should be the name of the Stars." We never again listened together to the Hollywood Stars.

It was that simple for Daddy, no ambiguity, no shades of gray, and no mitigating circumstances. A couple of decades after his death, in this era of corporate corruption, political chicanery, and athletes who lie, cheat, and steal, I often think of his old-fashioned principles, and how he tried to use sports as a metaphor to teach me about right and wrong. Not that Daddy would ever use a word such as *metaphor*.

Not long after he died, Mama told me he had never stopped talking about the day he took me to Gilmore Field and how upset he was about that legendary brawl. I reminded her that a few years later he escorted me to Chavez Ravine to see our newly relocated Dodgers.

I well remember both of those days. And I especially recall his words when we sat down to watch our beloved boys from Brooklyn.

"Now, Terri," he said, "You're going to see some class."

TERRI ELDERS, LCSW, in 2006 received the UCLA Alumni Award for Community Service for her work with the Peace Corps and AmeriCorps VISTA. She lives near Colville, Washington, with her husband, Ken Wilson. A lifelong writer and editor, her work has appeared in numerous newspapers, magazines, and anthologies.

His Way

ELYNNE CHAPLIK-ALESKOW

The strains of Sinatra singing "My Way" played over and over, as my father lay in front of the fireplace, tears rolling down his cheeks. He was grieving for the family-owned factory that had recently burned down and worrying about the family rift that resulted.

My father was strong enough to cry, but he did not believe in wallowing in personal pain. He made a plan, focused on his goal, and began the process of rebuilding. He offered his siblings the opportunity to join him, but they refused. They wanted the easy way out.

My paternal grandfather had founded the family business, and the image of the building and its contents in ashes had wrenched my father's heart. Of course he was going to rebuild it! He had his father's golden hands, hands that could build and invent anything.

At the time, my father was in his early fifties and had recently been diagnosed with colon cancer. But he was determined and put in grueling hours, day after day. Once he had made up his mind to rebuild, he never wavered from his mission to recreate his stainless steel polishing equipment line.

He was gone in the morning before we arose to prepare for school, and he came home at night long after we had gone to sleep. Seven days a week he followed this routine—painstakingly, and by himself—until he reconstructed the assembly line and got it back working. The physical labor alone could have broken a man half his age. When he had completed what his siblings told him could never be done, he found a buyer and prepared to sell the business.

My father had undergone surgery for colon cancer at the time his business became ashes, which meant the completion of the factory not only marked the success of his unique determination, but coincided with his being cancer-free. My dad envisioned a new life in which he and my mother would look toward semi-retirement. He had sent three of his four daughters to college, paid for one wedding, and only had one more daughter to set on a future path.

My father clearly identified with and loved "My Way" so much it became his signature song, bringing him solace and inspiration throughout this agonizing period of his life. The lyrics perfectly expressed his philosophy of living, and he generously bestowed this legacy as his gift to us. My father provided security for those he loved; he courageously trusted his talents and abilities. He displayed remarkable fortitude, industry, loyalty, and integrity—his way.

He told us, his four daughters, that family always came first and that his disappointment with some of his siblings was not to be our focus. Of course we knew that his pain would always be our pain. His tears were our tears. His strength was our hope. He was our father.

Shortly after he finalized the contract to sell the business he had rebuilt, my father prepared to fly to Florida with my youngest sister Ivy to meet my mother to celebrate the New Year. They were also celebrating my father being free of colon cancer. For my parents the future finally looked hopeful. Their dream of a shared tomorrow was in sight.

My father, Rubin Chaplik, was fifty-five years old when his plane crashed in Atlanta on the way to Florida killing him and my sixteen-year-old sister Ivy. The business contract was retrieved from the plane and thus ensured my mother's security in the twilight of her life.

Wherever and whenever my sisters or I hear "My Way", we stop, listen, and smile. Our father rebuilt his business for his family—and he did it his way. ✌

ELYNNE CHAPLIK-ALESKOW, Founding General Manager of WYCC-TV/PBS and Distinguished Professor Emeritus of Wright College in Chicago, is an author, public speaker, and award-winning educator and broadcaster. Her nonfiction stories and essays have been published in magazines and newspapers and are anthologized in *Chicken Soup for the Chocolate Lover's Soul, The Wisdom of Old Souls,* and *Forever Friends.* Future anthologies are in production. Visit Elynne at *http://LookAroundMe.blogspot.com.*

Stepping In

ELIZABETH KING GERLACH

While I was growing up, macho East Texas fathers typically spent their weekends eating too much *chili con queso* and screaming for their favorite football team. My stepdad, Ken, spent his weekends quietly exploring how varying light sources illuminate a bluebonnet.

Every weekend, in his makeshift studio—a room that served as a hallway between two rooms, which meant a constant flow of traffic, noise, and interruption—Ken diligently brushed delicate shades of color over white paper and pencil sketches. He was teaching himself how to paint with watercolor, which meant discarded paper cluttered his desk and the floor. "Studies" were tacked up on the wall and hung to dry on an indoor clothesline. How many ways can you paint a flower? On any given Sunday at our house, about 557 and counting. . . .

Ken worked a day job with the city and pulled in enough to "put bread on the table." But his true interest lay in painting bluebonnets or a still life—a loaf of bread and perhaps a glass of wine. He also loved music and taught us chords on the guitar. Many nights we would get together and listen to him pick bluegrass classics or strum folk songs. We learned how to sing along, even if we never quite became the next Von Trapp Family Singers.

It is only now, in retrospect, that I understand how much my stepdad undertook when he married my mom. She was a single mom when those two words weren't a familiar pairing, way back in the late 1960s. She had escaped an emotionally abusive husband, with three fragile little kids in tow, and was desperately trying to create a new life for herself—and for us.

Ken must have been crazy in love with her. (I'm pretty sure he still is.) They met in graduate school and were married outside near a lake, while wearing flowers in their hair. We kids baked them a Betty Crocker wedding cake that one lucky girl frosted and then used colored frosting to write "Mom + Ken = Love 4 Ever" across the top. I'm sure we fought over who got to do it.

My siblings and I vied for attention every minute of the day, and argued loudly over anything and everything, including interminable games of Monopoly. Someone inevitably stormed off at the end of the game, vowing to never play again. Nothing about our family life was either idyllic or perfect.

Somehow Ken managed to weather all the drama. Focusing on his art and music probably kept him sane. He loved art, and he loved to share his passion for it. He encouraged all of us to explore our creative sides, often insisting that we visit churches and museums where he taught us terms like *vernacular* and *fresco*. We also learned the meaning of inspiration. Ken filled our house with art books and moderated endless conversations that swung from genuine intellectual curiosity to comedic irony, such as, "Who was this Monet, and why couldn't he draw a straight line?"

My stepdad also helped me land my first job at a small newspaper when I was only fifteen. When I soon thereafter fell in love with writing and photography, Ken helped me set up my own dark room, took me to photo exhibitions, and explained the basics of composition and contrast.

Near the end of my senior year, I set my sights on entering a national photo competition. Still, as the deadline for the contest came down to the wire, I stalled when it came to completing the necessary steps to enter. I suffered from deep feelings of inadequacy and unworthiness, which meant that one day before the contest entries were due, I still had not mailed the photographs.

Maybe he had been holding back, waiting and watching for me to take responsibility, but finally, literally at the eleventh hour, Ken sat me down. "This is a big deal, and your work is good," he said. "I'm not going to let you blow this opportunity. There is such a thing as overnight mail, you know."

And that night he mailed the photos to the contest for me.

It was a small act of love, but a great act of faith. My photos won in several categories and ultimately I was awarded a college scholarship. To this day, I don't think that I would have had the confidence to become a writer if it wasn't for my stepdad literally stepping up and stepping in. His belief in me, even when I couldn't believe in myself, helped me gather confidence.

This would be heroic in itself, but it's not only his belief in me that makes him my hero. What I really admire is how he showed us all the importance of following your heart. Over the years, Ken's commitment to his art and his music won him many friends and awards; but it was his quiet persistence in following his own passion that inspired others to also follow theirs.

A good painting, like life, requires a delicate balance. Sometimes the flower is in the foreground, popping with color and stealing the show. Sometimes the flowers are in the field, acting as a supporting cast. Yes, my stepdad taught me that there are a thousand ways to see a flower, and when I needed him the most, he stepped in and showed me that *I was the flower.*

ELIZABETH KING GERLACH is the author of two award-winning books on autism. Her essays have appeared in various anthologies, including the *Cup of Comfort®* series. She lives with her family in Oregon. Learn more at *www.fourleafpress.com* (her stepdad's website is *www.kenaustin artist.com*).

Rediscovering Casanova

M. CAROLYN STEELE

Born in the hills of Arkansas, Dad was christened "Gath," after the city in the Bible where Goliath resided. If Grandma thought bestowing such a name insured height and boisterousness, she was disappointed. My short and gentle Dad was a teaser—a fact driven home my second day of kindergarten.

"It's true," I insisted to my teacher. "My daddy's name is Gath Casanova Fears." I was proud he wasn't an ordinary Bob, Joe, or John like the other children's fathers.

"Oh, surely not," my teacher managed to say through her laughter. She shook her head, "Your daddy's been teasing you, honey." I didn't learn the "C" actually stood for a pallid *Clarence* until a teenager, but I didn't blame him for fudging the truth. Dad claimed to be thirty-nine years old until the day he died at either the age of eighty-one or eighty-four. He'd fibbed about his birth date so often that no one knew the truth for sure.

If Dad wanted a male heir, we never knew it. He proclaimed nothing better than daughters and viewed all little boys as "hammerheads." Dad was a "piddler" by his own admission, which meant our backyard boasted a homemade swing set, dollhouse, and teeter-totter. In the days when dolls were breakable, he wired glass eyes back into doll heads and glued broken sections of wooden arms or legs together for all the girls in the neighborhood.

"Melba," he'd say to Mom at mealtime. "Another glass of iced tea, if you please." As soon as her back was turned, he'd wink and sneak bites of food I detested off my plate. From him, I learned chocolate chip cookies were best stolen hot off the pan behind the cook's back and not to look up with your mouth open if you were feeding seagulls at the beach.

A Sunday drive inevitably brought the command, "Girls, stick your tongue out at that yee-haw riding our back bumper. That'll teach him to keep a civil distance." We'd oblige amid much giggling, which delighted Dad and horrified my mother.

I was ten years old when my parents divorced and twelve when my sister went to live with my father. He wanted me, too, he said, and asked me to choose. But how does the first-born daughter leave her mother?

Shortly after "the choosing," Dad transferred from Corpus Christi to Lubbock, Texas, taking my sister with him. It was then I began shunning my father for he might as well have moved to the moon. He no longer came on Friday nights to take me to the drive-in where we'd see the latest western movie provisioned with homemade sugar cookies as big around as a coffee can—the only thing he could find to use as a cookie cutter.

Instead, he wrote letters, typed on tissue-thin paper describing the apartment with the pull-down bed and the wind that never stopped and the dust you tasted every time you went outside, and did I want to come live with him?

I folded the letter and never answered. How could I leave my mother?

Soon he wrote of the wonders of the Panhandle, the canyons and howling coyotes and cliff dwellings to explore, and did I want to come live with him?

I folded the letter and never answered. How could I leave my mother?

The year passed with a new letter every month, telling me of his job and the nice lady he met at church and did I want to come live with him? He would come for me any time I wanted.

I folded the letter and never answered. How could I leave my mother?

After Mom and I had moved for the umpteenth time, a letter written weeks earlier finally reached me. Dad wrote of the house he bought and the woman he married and now there would be a bedroom for me as well as my sister, and did I want to come live with him?

I folded the letter and resolved to never open another. Accepting Dad's remarriage was easier if I didn't know what was going on in his life. The stream of letters eventually slowed, but Christmas and birthday presents always arrived at my door. I walled the loss of my father off until one summer when he appeared unannounced and said to pack a suitcase; he was taking me on a vacation with his wife and my sister.

He was plumper and his eyes bluer than I remembered, but his smile was the same. I softened my resolve. It proved much too hard to both love and hate someone. Over the next few weeks we fished, explored caves, studied insects, climbed down ancient kivas, cooked over campfires, and in the process, I rediscovered my father.

I finally realized how much I had missed this simple camaraderie. I still couldn't bear to leave my mother, but letters flowed freely between my dad and I after that vacation. At first we argued the merits of who made the better cowboy, Roy Rogers or Gene Autry, or whether the most interesting part of history was the Civil War or the Old West. Eventually, the subject turned to school matters, career choices, and my discovery that not all boys were hammerheads.

My dad spoke only once in my adult life of his survival in the attack on Pearl Harbor which left him with damaged hearing. With typical humor, he capitalized on the infirmary. "Speak up, I can't hear you," he'd say with a chuckle when asked to do a chore. If you thought to short-circuit the standard reply and stand in front of him, he'd flip the newspaper, smile, and say, "Pretty busy here."

Years later, despite the ravages of aging, my father's gentle nature never deserted him. During one of his last hospitalizations, the old Casanova resurfaced when a nurse reached across his face to untangle IV lines and he gently kissed her arm.

"Oh, how sweet. A kiss," she said.

"Yes," Dad said, grinning, "you lucky woman, you."

Actually, Dad, I was the lucky one—lucky that you never gave up on me. ❧

M. CAROLYN STEELE retired from a career in commercial art to write and has garnered numerous awards and several published stories. She lives in Tulsa, Oklahoma, with her husband, who is definitely not a hammerhead, and still enjoys a good western accompanied by a stack of sugar cookies.

Wampum Doesn't Grow on Trees

ROBERT F. WALSH

I t was while riding atop a withered horse at a painfully slow trot through the cheering throngs packing either side of Main Street that I saw it. Leading my horse by the reins in the front of the Memorial Day Parade, dressed in full feathered headband and faux-leather Native American garb, was my dad: Big Bald Eagle.

And he was crying.

Not the flowing, girlish tears I'd cried earlier that day when I couldn't find my Third Year White Feather for my headband. No, my dad cried the subtle tears of that lone 1970s commercial Indian on the side of the road after seeing a driver toss garbage out the window. Even in that prepubescent moment of drunken adulation, astride my trusty steed and waving to the frenzied crowd in my Native American splendor, I was totally shocked.

My dad was not the type of man who shed tears.

Was he grieving about centuries of pain inflicted on the once-proud Native American nation? Was his pride swelling because his son had finally gotten a chance to ride one of the rented horses in our Indian Guide tribe in the parade? Or was he pained by the crushing irony of a third-generation Irishman and his son in head-to-toe face paint and feathers leading a parade that celebrated the military deaths of every American except the people we'd stolen the land from in the first place?

Turned out my dad was suffering from hay fever.

My dad was severely allergic to horses yet never said a word about it, even when I pleaded each year to be one of the riders in the parade. The slogan of the Indian Guides, a program for fathers and sons sponsored by the YMCA, was "Pals Forever." My father more than lived up to that.

An operations manager for General Electric with a wife and seven kids to feed, time was a precious commodity. Still, we never missed our bi-monthly Tuesday night gatherings of the tribe, a group consisting of nine hyperactive sixth graders and their bone-weary dads. The meetings would begin with the Chief asking one of us to beat the Tribal Drum, once for each of the four directions of the earth and for each boy present. After the prayer to the Great Spirit, the Wampum Bearer collected the tribal dues from each brave. My dad, brilliant with money, was the logical choice for Wampum Bearer.

Wampum was the money we were supposed to earn through our chores for the week, a kind of kiddy tithing we offered up to the tribe. Like the real world outside the tribe, it was an imperfect system. Dave Crowe's mom gave him five bucks allowance each week for doing nothing, while my dad parceled out my weekly twenty-five cents as if he were donating a kidney. As we placed our wampum in the Wampum Drum, we had to say how we earned it. Dave would mutter, "I took out the trash all week," even though we all knew his younger brother did. When I got up, my story sounded like a Red Cross disaster plan: "First, I repainted the bathroom radiators and put a new coat of varnish on the porch. Then, I cut up two cords of wood and stacked it under the deck for the winter. Next, I cleared the woods around our house of any fallen branches or dead trees. After that. . . ."

My older brother, Golden Eagle, would usually interrupt. "But did you *finish* cleaning the woods, Little Bald Eagle?" he'd ask.

You always had to tell the truth around the Sacred Circle. "I apologize to the tribe for being boastful," I'd reply, shooting daggers at Golden Eagle. The other braves would look awkwardly away, avoiding eye contact. *There but for the grace of the Great Spirit go I. . . .*

Once I asked for a raise in my allowance. "Wampum doesn't grow on trees," my dad replied sagely. He gave me an extra nickel a week. He could easily have caved in (like the rest of the dads), but he was teaching me something.

Next, each brave would grab the Talking Stick and give his Scouting Report, our progress toward the next Bead, Bear Claw, or Feather Class. After the old and new business (the *Indian Guide Handbook* says it all: "Keep all business short."), the centerpiece of each tribal meeting was arts and crafts. Some fathers went all out, spending hundreds of dollars on drum skins and balsam wood projects that would have put the Museum of Natural History to shame. One dad provided the makings for real tomahawks, and another proud papa provided each brave with a handcrafted totem pole to paint!

My dad showed us how to make a stick that, when rubbed, made a tiny propeller spin.

Not exactly a head-turner, but it fulfilled his tribal craft code: It took a long time to make, required little setup (and even less cleanup), and had a flashy name. The "Gee-Haw Whimmydiddle Stick" was the staple craft every time the Walsh family hosted the tribe. Craft time was followed by refreshment time, which consisted of screaming kids with Twinkies in their hands running around the caffeine-addled dads—just like real Indians!

I never knew that my dad had spent days researching how to build this Appalachian contraption—in the days before the Internet.

We'd close with a final prayer to the Great Spirit. I remember asking my dad why we prayed to Jesus on Sunday but to the Native American god on Tuesdays. "In your mind, just change *Great Spirit* to *Jesus*," he replied. Wow, I thought—if only those early Native Americans had known! This really could have saved them some trouble.

It's only now that I appreciate how much my dad did for us in our time in the Indian Guides. He showed his family what true sacrifice and commitment meant, refusing to miss meetings despite his exhaustion after long hours at work. He made his children a priority, even when it meant dressing in costume and face paint with a string of bear claws around his neck. He stood by me even as he sneezed and coughed his way down two excruciating miles on the Memorial Day Parade route. He never complained, because that's what big braves do for little braves. He did it my whole life.

I still have my headband. I still know the words to the "Pals Forever" camp song. As I think back on that day, it's my turn to shed some tears. My dad, Big Bald Eagle, is my pal forever. ✺

ROBERT F. WALSH writes in between the tides of his true passion: teaching. Even as his publishing credits grow, he is most proud of the fact that he has taught one of his cocker spaniels to *heel* on command. Rob, his wife, and two dogs live in Connecticut. Mr. Walsh's work has been published in, among others, *Pindeldyboz, Eclectica Magazine, Small Spiral Notebook,* and *Sweet Fancy Moses.* His nonfiction is included in the books, *In Our Own Words: A Generation Defining Itself,* Vol. 5 and Vol. 6.

More Than Mentors: Providential Dads

PRISCILLA CARR

Though neither contributed DNA, I consider two fine American poets, Robert Bly and Donald Hall, my providential fathers. One doesn't need genetic tissue to be adept and generous when it comes to offering fatherly attention—teaching, protecting, fostering growth, and loving someone. My biological dad was a mentally ill alcoholic who could never hold a job and was eventually taken away wrapped in a white jacket.

My biological dad did provide one gift: He taught me to read before I started kindergarten. My passion for words was birthed around our kitchen table. Dad recited Dickinson, Blake, and Longfellow, and then held contests to see which of us recited best. By first grade, I was beating him. Teachers asked, "How did you learn to do that?" But by then I was ashamed of my father so I lied and said I heard it on the radio. I loved Dad and knew he gave me what he could, but social shame proved a harsh reality.

Then, as well as later in life, I needed a stable, healthy father I could be *sure* of and who would make me proud to be his daughter. At fifty-six, I finally discovered such a dad in the poet Donald Hall. Don and I were both deeply grieving at the time: he for his wife and fellow poet, Jane Kenyon, and me for the murder of a fourteen-year-old in my husband's family. I wrote to him because I felt a psychic connection to Jane. When I explained that I was in the midst of a disabling onset of depression, Don responded by admitting he endured the same when he lost Jane. Thus began my mystical and poetical birthing, as Don Hall's "daughter."

Don mailed me a copy of Jane Kenyon's posthumous book *Otherwise*. "Since you had to get it on interlibrary loan, I thought you might like your own copy." The book arrived on Christmas Eve, and since my dad seldom remembered a birthday and was always drunk on holidays, this gift, and its timing, meant more to me than Don could ever realize. Don's paternal love proved as steady as his friendship. Through him, I met the poet Robert Bly, his friend for sixty years, since first meeting at Harvard.

At Don's suggestion, I attended Robert's reading at the University of New Hampshire in 2003. When Robert mentioned that he often mentored young writers, I boldly asked, "Do you help out not-so-young, just-starting-out poets and writers?"

Robert smiled, "Oh, sure. What do you have in mind?"

We talked for a while, and then I said, "We have a friend in common."

"Who might that be?" Robert's eyes danced behind his glasses.

"Donald Hall."

"I am staying at Don's place tonight. Who shall I say is claiming to be his friend?"

Three years later, I attended Robert's annual "Great Mother Conference," a gathering of artists who inspire, instruct, and support each other. In private moments, Robert and I discussed his friendship with Jane Kenyon and Donald Hall, but the focus of the conference was workshops, poetry salons, and master classes. In the tradition of a master teacher, Robert read daily and interacted with his audience. He also attended workshops as our peer and gleefully learned from presenters. It's small wonder that Robert's community of artists loves him.

Friendships formed at Great Mother Conferences led me to attend Bill Moyers's Tribute to Robert Bly at the 92nd St. Y in New York City in honor of his eightieth birthday. A month later, Robert and I spoke at Galway Kinnell's eightieth. At the Block Island Poetry Project, Robert and I discussed the construction of prose poems, and he asked, "Why do you keep showing up at these events?"

"I come because of you, Robert." His eyes peered into mine.

Despite the major part he played in the coming together of thousands through these conferences, Robert is the opposite of inflated—he feels humble in the face of the largesse of creation and grateful for opportunities to inspire or commune with fellow writers. I reaffirmed, "It's all because of *you*. Because of the way you have helped me feel a part of your Great Mother Family." Again, Robert silently looked into my eyes, bowed slightly, and left the dining room.

Over the last few years, Robert and I have exchanged letters, shared talks about Jane Kenyon, and spoken intimately about his relationship with his father and his friendship with Don Hall. When my husband and I watched Robert weep at Great Mother, as he read poetical elegies to his dad, we were greatly moved. It was hard for me to imagine a father figure who would tenderly ask for sidelights to be put on, "So I can peer into all those beautiful faces out there that I know . . . and love."

Since my friendship with Don and Robert had opened my heart to the love a healthy father figure can offer, I encouraged my forty-year-old son, who manages Asperger's syndrome and a movement disorder, to attend one of Robert's men's conferences in Minnesota. I was thrilled when my son returned a kinder, more expressive man, just as Robert promised, and rejoiced in feeling as if Robert also—knowingly or unknowingly—fulfills the role of a God-sent grandfather to our son.

Don and Robert provide master class education, encouragement, and the bonus of hugs and kisses. I feel commissioned to act as their personal ambassador of affections as I transport hugs and kisses to and from the other in my various venues with each. I prize intimate photos with Don and Robert, and their notes of congratulations for my modest publications.

My continuing personal correspondence with Don and attendance at Robert's Great Mother Conferences are a profound joy, proving that it never is too late to become a member of a happy family. These two fine poets may not realize that I view them as my fathers, but they *are*. I love them and am very proud of them. It matters not whether we share strands of DNA. What matters is that each of us carries the other in our hearts and each is *sure* of the other . . . ever. ✥

PRISCILLA CARR'S memoir vignette, "The Major" appears in *A Cup of Comfort® for Dog Lovers* and her story "Launches from a Paper World" is in the anthology *My Teacher Is My Hero*. Her husband Richard is her muse.

A Winter's Tale

DAVID W. BAHNKS

Our weatherman on the evening news warned that we were under a severe winter storm warning in Northern Illinois. What better time to stay home and hibernate by the fire? The howling wind outside my window sparked a memory of another time—almost seventy years ago—when the old Grim Reaper came for me swinging his scythe. My father had to fend him off with his sword and shield.

After adding logs to the fire, I nestled in my recliner with a cup of hot cocoa. Sliding the family album across my lap, I searched for my favorite photo of the old patriarch—a tintype of Pa in his twenties standing next to Ma in her Victorian-style wedding dress.

He appeared tall and gallant with his bowler hat cocked forward on his head, wearing a dark suit with a crisp, white collar and black tie. He had a neatly trimmed handlebar mustache, and his eyes . . . yes . . . there was that twinkle—the kind of sparkle you get when you know a secret or something exciting, but you weren't quite ready to tell.

Eyes closed, I let my memory drift back to that time when I had the flu and the beginning of pneumonia. Pa carried me from my bed into the parlor and held me on his lap. "How goes it, little man," he asked in his deep, gravelly voice. "Feelin' better?"

He had just come in from the barn and still wore his leather coat. Oh, how I loved to nuzzle the sheepskin of his lapel and smell the imbued cigar smoke. "No, Pa," I wheezed, struggling for every breath.

With a nod, he laid me on the couch and propped my head with several pillows then took my temperature with his lips pressed on my forehead.

I could sense his fear and determination from his wide, pale-blue eyes, since the closest doctor lived in Moline—about thirty miles from our place. Being self-sufficient like most folks in those times, my parents used the remedies handed down through the generations—turpentine for abrasions, homemade salve for burns or insect bites, and castor oil for constipation. Only this time, I had begun to suffocate from the phlegm gathering in my chest, and we were in the middle of a raging blizzard with drifts high as the roof.

Noticing Pa's furrowed brow, it was plain to see that he knew he would be in for a long, hard night—especially with Ma already showing symptoms of the disease.

Pa rubbed goose grease on my chest and covered the sticky layer with a hand-knitted, woolen mat. To humidify the room, he put a pan containing a mixture of water and some smelly stuff that made my sinuses sting on the Franklin stove. He then made a tent out of a sheet to direct the medicated steam to my wheezing, gurgling lungs. I struggled for every breath and could barely stay awake. I'm sure Pa figured that if I were to fall asleep, I'd give up and quit breathing. To keep me stimulated, he dabbed my forehead with a cold, wet cloth and told me about our ancestors who settled in Illinois.

"These stories were passed along from father to son," he began. "The first folks to settle on our farm were two brothers from Sundsvall, Sweden, in the late 1700s. They both brought citified wives from New York. The living was too tough, so both women gave up and moved back east."

I reclined against the pillows and listened to Pa's fascinating story, accompanied by my labored breath and the chiming of Grandpa's cast-iron clock on the bookcase. Each breath I took felt like an agonizing step up a steep mountain toward the summit. But, I found his raspy voice comforting and the story of our origin fascinating—they kept me struggling to stay alive.

"Well, Son," he continued, "those two traded several horses for two Chippewa Indian women—both hearty as a dang mule. One of them took to the farm life well. She's your great-great grandma. But the other one turned out to be mean—a regular she-cat, that one."

"What happened to her, Pa?" I asked.

"Well, old Homer told everyone the woman run off, but some trappers found her floatin' face down in the Rock River without a mark on her."

"Think old Homer did it?" I asked.

He waited until my gasps for air subsided. "Nobody ever knew for sure. And there weren't any lawmen 'round here in those days. God-fearin' folk just took care of their own problems in their own way. Nope, old Homer went and found him another Indian wife and had a dozen kids."

Pa went on telling me one story after another until well into the night. Occasionally, he'd duck into the bedroom to check on Ma or toss a lump of coal on the fire, but he'd come right back and continue. Through the window, I saw the sunrise through the winter skeletons of oaks along the eastern hedgerow and I knew I would make it okay. I could see the relief on Pa's face when he mopped the sweat from my neck and face when my fever broke. He obviously knew that his efforts paid off; that old Grim Reaper wouldn't be harvesting his only son as long as he was around to do him battle.

During the next few days, Pa continued the struggle to pull Ma through her illness. I had all the confidence in the world that he would make her well, and he did.

Pa went on to serve his country during the big war. I'll never forget the pride I felt the day he came home and stepped off the train in his army uniform. I had often imagined his involvement in some heroic invasion, but he never spoke about those times.

Through the years that followed his death, I remember being awakened by the winter wind with the feeling that something warm had touched my forehead. I know this makes me sound crazier than a pet raccoon, but I swear I could feel a presence hovering over me in the darkness of my room. I even detected a faint scent of cigar smoke. Who knows, maybe old Pa's spirit has something to do with my surviving to this ripe old age. ❧

DAVID W. BAHNKS is a member of the Oklahoma Writers Federation, Ozark Writer's League, Arkansas Ridge Writers, and Arkansas River Valley Writers Association. David studied creative writing at the University of Arkansas, and is published in two historical anthologies about the Ozarks.

Well, I've Had a Plenty!

LAWRENCE D. ELLIOTT

"Welcome to San Diego," the captain's voice greeted as the plane slowly taxied in. I breathed in a lung full of air to quell the swell of emotions. I was finally home.

I grabbed my small carry-on, straightened my dress blue uniform that I would wear for the last time, and stood in the aisle with the other passengers—like cattle—waiting to be released, shifting from leg to leg until the doors were finally opened. Surprised by the surge of emotions, I tried to gather my thoughts, tried to catch my breath as the intensity of finally re-entering civilian life overcame me.

I walked through the airport glancing at each person, longing to see a familiar face—an old school buddy or someone I played ball with—anyone, as long the face was familiar.

Reaching the baggage area, I grabbed my suitcase as it made its serpentine path through the system. As I exited the terminal, there he was, standing next to his station wagon, sporting a smile on his granite-like face, his hands tucked in his back pockets.

"Hi," my grandfather said as we embraced.

"Hi, L," I replied.

Stepping back, he looked up at the blue beret perched on my head saying, "You have to wear that hat?"

"Why," I asked smiling. "What's wrong with it?"

"Nothing, I guess," he said taking my bag. In one motion, he opened the door and flung it in. I sat on the passenger side, placing my carry-on on the floor. My grandfather got in, started the car, and slowly pulled away.

He was born in the small Louisiana town of Lillie in 1922 as "L Hawthorne" and was the only person I'd ever known who had a single letter for a name. And I wasn't alone. Whenever he met someone new, they'd ask what it stood for. He'd always reply with a polite smile, "L, just L."

One day, I asked, "How come you only have one letter as your name?"

The answer was something I've never forgotten.

When he was born, a man in the parish decided on his name. And even though his parents may not have liked it, the times would not allow them to object or change it. It was the segregated South. The man was white. My grandfather's parents were black.

"Larry," he said calmly, "in those days, when a white man named you, you stayed named." I was in my militant teen years at the time, so I found it infuriating. He, on the other hand, seemed devoid of anger or bitterness. Noticing his demeanor had calmed me. His face said it all: *Baby, it was just the way things were.*

After serving in the Navy during World War II, this man known only as L took my grandmother and my mother to California seeking better opportunities. Working various odd jobs to support the family, he finally landed a secure job with the city of San Diego, where he faithfully worked for thirty-one years repairing the worn streets of the city. He was never late and rarely sick. In 1961, I became the first in our line to become what seems a rare creature—a native Californian.

Even though he and my grandmother were always in our lives, my grandfather took on an even more prominent role when my father decided he no longer wanted the responsibility of a family and moved on. When other mothers were shedding tears over lost sons to the all-too-often deadly influences of the street, my mother did everything she could to not let that happen. But it was my grandfather who provided that all-important positive male figure in my life.

As we made our way down the highway, my grandfather leaned over and said, "On our way we'll stop at the county recorder's office."

"Oh, do you need to pick something up?" I asked.

"No," he answered, "you need to record your discharge papers."

"Hmm," I thought.

When I processed out of the Air Force an old master sergeant gave me one final piece of advice. "Young man, when you get home, don't forget to record your DD214. You never know, you might lose it." He went on to say, "It's tough to get a new one."

It had slipped my mind, but, as always, my grandfather knew what had to be done.

"*How* did he know that?" I thought while staring out the window, reacquainting myself with home.

So, we made a quick stop at the recorder's office and took care of business.

Soon we were on the road again. As we made our way down the slightly changed, yet familiar streets, passing by a few of the landmarks from my past, an *Oh, Yeah* filled my soul. We drove by the Little League field where my grandfather took me to my first practice. This, incidentally, was around the corner from the church I had known since birth. My heart was warming up as I marveled at how a place can change in just four years, yet still stay relatively the same. Occasionally, the passing scenery would prompt me to ask about various friends. During the ride I would learn of who was in jail, who was dead, and who was on "the drugs," as my grandfather would say. I stared out the window as I listened to the sad tales of wasted lives. Did they have a man like my grandfather in their lives? Did they not have the example I had of how hard work, determination, and character can smooth out even the most rugged path?

Arriving at my mother's home, my grandfather let me in, and then, ensuring I had all I needed, he left me to await her return. I sat my bags in a corner of the living room, melted into the comfortable couch, and drifted off to sleep. Soon, I was awakened by the sounds of my mother working in the kitchen. I stood up and stretched, a wide smile gathering.

"Hi," I said. "Well I'm home."

"Yes you are," my mother replied. Emotions surging, we hugged and kissed each other.

As each member of the family trickled in for a family dinner, more emotional greetings ensued. Soon, we were all standing around the dinner table, holding hands and bowing our heads while my grandfather said grace. It was just as I had remembered it.

"Amen," he ended. As I looked down, I relished a welcome sight: a spread of chicken, candied yams, collard greens, and marshmallow salad. And of course, there was my grandfather's sweet potato pie. The chow hall never looked like this.

As we all dug in, everyone shot questions at me.

"What are your plans?" asked one person.

"What's the next step?" asked another.

"Are you going back to school?" yet another asked.

At that point, I didn't have any answers. I just wanted to revel in this moment of being home; of finally being with the people who meant the most to me. Those answers could wait until tomorrow.

.   After finishing his meal, my grandfather plopped down on the couch and let out a sigh, just as he always had after a family meal. "Well," he exclaimed in his customary fashion, "I've had a plenty!"

Thinking back, I did, too.

LAWRENCE D. ELLIOTT is a nationally published author and Realtor® in Southern California. His work has been included in many popular books including *Chicken Soup for the Soul*. He lives with his wife Lisa and his dog Lacie in Ontario. View his work on *www.LawrenceElliott.com*.